To Partake of Tea

THE LAST LADIES OF KINGSTON LACY

Geoffrey Brown

First published in the United Kingdom in 2006 by
The Hobnob Press, PO Box 1838, East Knoyle, Salisbury SP3 6FA

British Library Cataloguing in Publication Data
A catalogue record for this book is available from the British Library.

ISBN10   0-946418-50-0
ISBN13 (from January 2007) 978-0-946418-50-3

Typeset in 11/15 pt Georgia
Typesetting and origination by John Chandler
Printed in Great Britain by Salisbury Printing Company Ltd, Salisbury

Contents

Acknowledgements

MY THANKS to Kate Warren, Collection Manager; Nigel Chalke, Garden and Countryside Manager; Rob Gray, House Steward; to Carolyn Anand, Volunteer Researcher and Nick Curtis all at Kingston Lacy. To James Grasby, Curator (Interiors) of the Wessex Region, The National Trust for his help and support and to Martin Papworth, Wessex Region Archaeologist, particularly for his assistance with Chapter 2, *Walter Ralph Bankes*. Also to Sue Hardy, one time Head Gardener at Kingston Lacy now a Director of Orchard Park, Gillingham, Dorset. I am grateful to the National Trust for granting me permission to reproduce the illustrations on pages 7, 10, 19, 20, 25, 61 and 67.

Thank you, the Staff of the Dorset History Centre, Dorchester for their professionalism and patience when guiding me through the extensive Bankes Archives. (ref. D/BKL). To Lt. Col. T.C.E. Vines Rtd. of the Prince of Wales Own Regiment of Yorkshire for providing the background material to Hilary's father's Army career and to Mrs. Jill Brett for her patient reading of, and constructive comments on the draft text.

To The Lord and Lady Digby, of Minterne Magna for kindly allowing me access to Lady Beryl Digby's Diaries covering the early part of the 20th Century and to Capt. and Mrs. Thimbleby of Wolveton House for their help. To Bishop Michael Marshall of Holy Trinity Church, Sloane Street, London; Mrs. Vera Ricketts, Church Warden of St. Stephen's Church, Pamphill; Mrs. Diane Nolte, formally of Pamphill Manor; Miss Mary Wills of the Corfe Castle Trust and to Mrs. Penny Copland-Griffiths for all their help and support.

To Mr. Philip Chissell of Cowgrove Farm, Mr. and Mrs. Angus Purchase of New Barn Farm, Mr. Jim Richards of Chilbridge Farm, and to

Mr. Rob James of Bothenwood Farm. Also my thanks to Mrs. Marge Cherrett, Mrs. Pat Hughes, Mrs. Anne Sugden, and Mrs. Pam Fiander.

Many thanks, also to Mr. and Mrs. Philip Lodder, together with Mrs. Daphne Harris and Mrs. Christine Turner for giving of their time and being so helpful with their reminiscences. To Mr. Rupert Russell, the owner of Wassand Hall. To Mrs. Sybil Rhodes, whose late husband Eric and his father were Agents to the Bankes' Estate, for making available photographs also giving generously of her time to provide much background material for the research. Thanks also to Mr. and Mrs. Julian Payne of Burton Bradstock, for making freely available to me family documents and photographs, Julian's father being the Bankes' Chauffeur prior to the 2nd World War.

Finally I would like to express my deep appreciation to all those people, although not mentioned here who have simply offered words of appreciation, support and encouragement together with all those organizations who have invited me to address them at their meetings and beg their forgiveness for not referring to them by name.

In conclusion I would like to thank my wife Jean for giving me the time and space simply 'to get on with it'.

Geoffrey Brown

Bibliography

Bankes, Viola, *Why Not?* (Jarrolds, 1934)

Bankes, Viola, *A Dorset Heritage: the Story of Kingston Lacy* (Richards Press, 1953; 2nd. edition, Anthony Mott Ltd., 1986)

Bankes, Viola and Watkins, Pamela, *A Kingston Lacy Childhood* (Dovecote Press, 1986)

Bankes, Wynne Albert, Diaries, 1860 - 1913 (Dorset History Centre, Dorchester ref. D/181)

Mitchell, Anthony, *Kingston Lacy* (National Trust Guide Book, 1994)

Bankes Archive (Dorset History Centre, Dorchester ref. D/BKL)

Introduction

THIS IS A GLIMPSE into the lives of two ladies, Mrs. Henrietta Jane, or Jenny, Bankes and Mrs. Hilary Margaret Bankes, both of Kingston Lacy.

As we shall see in the forthcoming chapters, Henrietta Jane was the mother of Henry John Ralph Bankes, or Ralph as he preferred to be called, and Hilary Margaret, his wife. Ralph was the last of a long line of Bankes who owned the Kingston Lacy and Corfe Castle Estate, the family tracing its ownership back to the early 17th century. Upon his death in 1981 Ralph bequeathed the Estate to The National Trust, although it was not until 1983 that The Trust formally accepted ownership.

I have tried to relate the story of Mrs. Henrietta Bankes' and Mrs. Hilary Bankes' lives as they might have told it, with perhaps reference to family scrap books and photo albums, to their children or possibly their grandchildren, in the Day Nursery overlooking the terrace and lawn of Kingston Lacy. But as we shall see this family picture was not as it appears at first glance. As with many families pressures from within and without, together with decisions made, or not made, transpired to bring the fabric of the Estate almost to the point of being beyond repair. It was only with hard work by everyone involved, together with the Estates' considerable financial resource, brought together by the expertise of The National Trust, was it saved for us to enjoy for ever.

Although it is a family home no more, Kingston Lacy House still has that warm atmosphere with lamps lighting the dark corners and fresh flowers on many of the tables. As one visitor was heard to say, 'you feel that the family have just gone out for a while and will soon be back'.

Since the Trust took over in 1983 a large number of tenants have continued to work on the Estate, adding to the valuable fund of knowledge acquired over the centuries. Continuity with the past is important for it enables us to understand better the thoughts, decisions and actions of our predecessors, and more particularly in the case of this book, Mrs. Henrietta Bankes and Mrs. Hilary Bankes.

In applying the titles of Mrs. to the names of our two ladies of Kingston Lacy together with other titles and the use of grammatical phrases that have gone out of fashion, I hope to recreate some of the atmosphere of the periods described. Additionally, quotations from some of the newspaper reports of events taking place at the time will, I hope, also help to paint a picture in words of the day to day life of the Nation. This story of the last two Ladies of Kingston Lacy is therefore a snapshot of the gradual disappearance of the country squire, his wife, and their lifestyle.

All is not doom and gloom for estates such as Kingston Lacy. Although living in a world where 'ordinary' people have a greater opportunity to have their say in the decisions that affect their lives, The National Trust has, at times, more than its fair share of critics. However, only a powerful organisation such as the Trust, with its loyal membership, can stand against some of the unscrupulous developers and people buying properties as holiday homes and only using them for a very few weeks in the year. Imagine the impact on such beautiful villages as Pamphill and Cowgrove had the Estate gone up for sale in 1981 to pay the necessary death duties when Ralph Bankes died.

Today we can walk around Kingston Lacy House, the garden and the Estate and see for ourselves the impact that Mrs. Henrietta Bankes had on the area, but we can only speculate on how the Estate would look today had Mrs. Hilary Bankes not died so early.

Although the two ladies 'reigned' for approximately the same number of years there is very little to be seen of Hilary's influence on the Estate, however I hope that this book will give the reader a greater understanding of why that is so, and how the Kingston Lacy and Corfe Castle Estate developed during the 20th Century, together with the achievements and disappointments of the two last Ladies of Kingston Lacy.

1
The Frasers

As STATED in the Introduction, Henry John Ralph Bankes, or Ralph as he preferred to be known, died in 1981 and was the last owner of the Kingston Lacy and Corfe Castle Estate. Henrietta Jane, or as she was more usually known, Jennie Bankes, née Fraser, was his Mother.

Henrietta's great-grandfather was Alexander Fraser, who was born on 21st November 1775 in Inverness, and married in Aberdeen on 31st May 1798, Agnes Dingwall Fordyce on the occasion of her 17th birthday.

Alexander, who was described as being 'warm hearted, genial in disposition and processed of a great fund of humour,' carried on business in Aberdeen as a merchant, corn factor and ship owner, and became Provost of Aberdeen about 1815. There are portraits of both Alexander and Agnes hanging in the Day Nursery at Kingston Lacy House, Dorset.

Agnes and Alexander had five sons and seven daughters. John Mathison, their second child, was born on the 21st November 1805, the first, a son having been born in 1801, died in 1805.

On 23rd September 1833 John Mathison married Gertrude Eleonore Nottebohm, daughter of the Baron Nottebohm of Antwerp, but six months after John and Gertrude were married in Antwerp, John's mother, Agnes, died on 6th March 1834 aged 53, which sadly meant she did not live long enough to see any of her grandchildren. However, Alexander, John's father, lived to the age of sixty-five and died in Aberdeen on 21st May 1840.

Between the years 1835 and 1849 John Mathison and Gertrude had six children, all born in Antwerp. They were:

Alexander Casper born 22nd June 1835

Lydia Marianne, b 1837

William Thomson, b 14th October 1841

Arthur Abraham, b 1843

Edward Seymour, b 1847 and

John Christian, b 1849

Their father, John Mathison, died in his 80th year on 13th January 1885, at Palace House, Paddington. His sister, Angelica Patience, was present at the time of his death. We do not know when or where his wife, Gertrude Eleanor, died, but it was before 1st November 1887, as we can see from a wall tablet in Mongewell Church which reads:

IN LOVING MEMORY OF

JOHN MATHISON FRASER AND GERTRUDE ELEONORE EMILIE

NOTTEBOHM HIS WIFE

THIS WINDOW IS DEDICATED BY THEIR CHILDREN ALEXANDER CASPER,

LYDIA MARIANNE, ARTHUR ABRAHAM AND JOHN CHRISTIAN,

NOVEMBER 1ST 1887.

Alexander Casper Fraser, their first born, married in 1856, Maria Johanna Thaden (b 8th October 1834, d 7th July 1907), presumably in Rotterdam, as she was the only child of Bernard Thaden of Rotterdam. They had at least one son, 'with other issue', John Mathison (b 1867).

From a photocopy of a page made available to me and taken from an unidentified publication we learn that;

Alexander Casper Fraser bought from the Price family, the Mongewell Estate, near Wallingford, now in Oxfordshire, this also included 13 Sussex Square (London W). Over the next few years he made considerable changes. The lodge at the top of the drive was built; the 'old' boathouse was constructed beside the Thames and the Church was improved. Within two years of Alexander Casper buying the Estate, a new house had been completed – Mongewell Park. The old house was therefore pulled down.

All these changes must have cost a great deal of money; but the Frasers seemed to have been very prosperous. (In 1883) two years before he died Alexander Casper's father, John Mathison, spent lavishly on the occasion of his Golden Wedding Anniversary: money was given to several hundred poor people in Wallingford, presents were sent to those in the Cottage Hospital and a special tea was provided for Wallingford school children; while in the evening there was a grand party at Mongewell with lanterns around the grounds, gondolas on the Thames and a firework display to finish. Like his father Alexander Casper could be generous to those less fortunate than himself. He is on record as having paid for an outing of local children and as having contributed towards the local celebrations in 1911 to mark the Coronation of King George V.

Alexander Casper took seriously his responsibilities as a leader of the community. He was a Justice of the Peace and a Deputy to the Lord Lieutenant, responsible for law and order in the County.

In 1916 Alexander Casper died. His body was placed next to his wife's near Mongewell Church. By then the First World War had been raging for two years and for the next two years Mongewell Park became a hospital for wounded officers.'

During the 2nd World War Mongewell Park was the home of a Medical Rehabilitation Unit for Royal Australian Air Force men who had been severely injured whilst on active service in Europe. A painting by Stella Bowen, which can be viewed on the Australian War Memorial website, shows:

> . . . amputees or those who have been otherwise maimed, enjoying and afternoon of archery or golf as they await repatriation to Australia.

John Mathison and Gertrude Eleonore Fraser's third child was William Thomson, born on 14th October 1841 in Antwerp. In 1865, at the age of 23, he married Anna Hermina Sophia Cornelia Onnen, in Sourabaya, Java, where, from various documents we learn that he was a 'merchant', presumably in the spice trade. They had two children whilst living in Java: Henrietta Jane, born on 21st May 1867 in Sourabaya, and John Thomson born 6th September 1869 in Samarang.

Five days after Henrietta was born, and in England, Princess May of Teck later to become Queen Mary was born. Some readers may remember Queen Mary and the stiff austere image that surrounded her.

It is worth keeping that image in the back of our minds when we try to appreciate some of Henrietta's style, attitudes and decisions.

During the early 1870s, William Thomson was variously acting unpaid Consul and Vice Consul in Batavia and Samarang on behalf of the British Foreign Office, and was Chairman at a number of meetings of British residents in Batavia between 1870 and 1871.

It must have been in the late 1870s that William Thomson, together with his wife Anna and their two children, Henrietta and John, arrived in London. On 4th March 1880 Anna gave birth to her third child, a sister for Henrietta and John, but it was nearly five weeks before William Thomson registered the birth of Jessie Maud Fraser. Two months later on 31st May 1880 at the age of 38, William Thomson Fraser died at the family home, 27 Pembridge Square, Kensington, London, of (according to the death certificate) 'glandular inflammation of the neck and fatty degeneration of the heart'. Thomas Ransom of the same address was present at his death. Henrietta was 13 years old, her brother 10½ and Jessie about three months. No further information regarding their mother, Anna has so far come to light.

Our story moves on to 1893, when it would appear from Bankes archive material held in Kingston Lacy House, that Henrietta, her brother John and possibly Jessie were in Germany.

Amongst the archives are a number of 'Invitations to Balls' addressed to 'Mr. John and Miss Fraser' together with a letter dated 17th January 1893 from an address in Berlin:

> Dear Mr. Fraser
> I have received commands to say that the Emperor Frederick would like to see you and your sister before His Majesty leaves . . . for England. Would you and your sister write your names in His Majesty's Book and could your sister leave a card on Countess Birchl (?)
> Sincerely G. Leckhurst.

Additionally in the archives are photographs of a number of cities and towns in Belgium, France, Germany, Switzerland and the Channel Islands. Further material indicates that Henrietta visited Hamburg in 1895.

Henrietta, Jessie and John Fraser, c. 1890 (National Trust)

Photographs of Henrietta, her brother John and sister Jessy show their features to be wholly European, and one can only speculate whether there were any qualities in Henrietta's speech that gave some clue to her Far Eastern birth and 'Colonial' upbringing. We should bear in mind that, until they had arrived in London, probably in the late 1870s, none of the family would have heard the English language as it would have been spoken by people resident in Britain.

For anyone who saw themselves as part of the upper echelons of society, the one occasion of the year not to be missed was the 'London

Season'. It would seem that Henrietta, although untitled and from an untitled family, was very much involved in that social scene – to such effect that it completely changed the life of one middle-aged bachelor from Dorset, together with many hundreds of other people. Her impact can still be seen today.

2

Walter Ralph Bankes

OUR STORY now moves to the Kingston Lacy and Corfe Castle Estate in Dorset, the home of Walter Ralph Bankes.

This large estate covers sixteen and a half thousand acres and it has been said that the history of the estate reflects the history of England with features dating back at least 10,000 years. These range from the Mesolithic remains underlying the Iron Age hill-fort at Badbury Rings, through to the Roman period with much evidence of the farms, settlements and field systems occupied at that time. For the Medieval period, the extensive archaeological evidence is enhanced by contemporary documents preserved in the Bankes family archive.

The Bankes' dynasty started with Sir John and Dame Mary. Sir John rose to be Chief Justice of the Common Pleas during the reign of King Charles I. Corfe Castle, being the Bankes' family home, was subjected to two sieges by the parliamentarian troops during the Civil War. Dame Mary, wife of Sir John, became a royalist figurehead in the brave defence of her home against overwhelming odds. The garrison was eventually betrayed by one of the defenders who allowed sixty parliamentarian soldiers in through a side gate, thus enabling the stronghold to be captured. 'Brave' Dame Mary, as she became more popularly known, was allowed to leave the Castle, with the keys. Her husband, Sir John, having died in Oxford, she subsequently returned to her own family home in Ruislip. The keys to the Castle now hang in the library at Kingston Lacy House.

The parliamentarian troops then set about destroying the Castle, and the ruins you see today are the results of this slighting. What happened to the contents of the Castle is a matter of speculation.

The story of the siege of Corfe Castle is told in David Thackray's comprehensive Corfe Guide Book and, together with the story of the Kingston Lacy Estate by Anthony Mitchell, is recommended reading.

The house at Kingston Lacy was built by Sir John and Lady Bankes' second son, Sir Ralph Bankes, between 1663 and 1665, but the house you see today is very different to the original design, having been subjected to much reconstruction and refurbishment. In the 1830s William John Bankes transformed the house, the most dramatic internal change being the installation of the marble staircase which he designed and had built in Carrare, Italy, and shipped to England.

Following William John's ownership, the estate continued to evolve and be developed by subsequent members of the Bankes family although in a somewhat less dramatic way.

Walter Ralph Bankes was born on 23rd July 1853, the second son of Edmund George Bankes and his wife Rose Louise née Bastard, Henry John Percival being the eldest. Edmund had a number of brothers, two of whom were Cornet William George Hawtrey Bankes VC who died of his wounds at Lucknow, India in 1858; and, Wynne Albert Bankes of whom we shall hear more later. Henry and Walter also had a sister, Adelaide Annie, who was born on 2nd October 1856. Sadly tragedy struck when, being carried down to meet her parents she fell out of the arms of a nurse or governess on to the marble staircase, and her spine was permanently damaged. She lived at Kingston Lacy up to the time of Walter's marriage, then went to live at 9 Wilton Place, Belgravia, London and died, aged 53 on 1st November 1909. She is buried in Studland churchyard along with many other members of the Bankes family.

Walter inherited the estate in 1869, on the death of his brother Henry John Percival Bankes. One of the most visible items of Walter's ownership is the superb stable block, designed by T. H. Wyatt and completed in 1880. Another is the establishment, in 1895, of the herd of Red Devon Cattle, which is still very much part of the scene in the park at Kingston Lacy. Additionally during this period Walter had electricity

Walter Ralph Bankes (National Trust)

installed in Kingston Lacy House.

Walter also had built the kitchen garden complete with extensive greenhouses, but being some way from the House criticism was levelled at him for not having them located on a site that was more readily accessible. These gardens are tenanted and not, at the time of publication, open to the general public.

Up until the time of Henry's death, Walter had little or no responsibilities and therefore spent much of his life indulging in travelling, horse racing, various country pursuits, and, we are led to believe, plenty of 'wine, women and song'. This lifestyle made him very popular both out in the countryside and in the social scene of London at the end of the 19th century. It was even noted in the London *Evening Standard* during November 1892 that:

> Mr. Ralph Bankes whilst shooting with Major Brymer MP at Puddletown was struck in the eye with shot, necessitating a journey to town to consult a specialist.

Although untitled, he was also probably, very popular with many matchmaking mothers anxious that their daughters should marry up the social ladder. But, to use a horse racing parlance, they were 'beaten to the post' by Miss Henrietta Jane Fraser.

3
The Marriage of Henrietta and Walter

NOT HAVING BEEN ABLE to locate any diaries that Henrietta or Walter may have kept, how and where they met is unclear, but it would seem that it may have been difficult for them not to have met. A detached diary page for June, the year not recorded, found in a Bankes archive box in the Dorset History Centre, Dorchester, gives some idea of the social life during 'The Season' in London at the end of the 19th Century. During the month in question, the writer of the diary, presumably Walter, received eleven invitations to attend balls; seven for luncheons; four for dinners; three for dancing; one for music and five for other social occasions. He also spent one week of that month in Dorset!

Wolveton House, Dorchester (author, by kind permission of Capt. Thimbleby)

At this point another important player comes into the story. Wynne Albert Bankes who was the youngest brother of Walter's father, in other words, Walter's uncle.

In an entry in his diary for 23rd June 1897, Albert Bankes, as he was usually known, writes:

> I was walking in the Park . . . When (Walter) Ralph my Nephew introduced me to Miss Jennie Fraser whom he met on Monday June 14th and proposed to on Saturday June 19th.

We also learn from his diary that two days later, 25th June, Albert and his wife Florrie went, 'To Kingston Lacy for the day where we found Jennie Fraser, her sister Jessie and her brother Jack'; and the entry for 3rd July, 'Ralph and Miss Fraser arrived for two nights.' This was at Albert and Florrie's home, Wolfeton House near Dorchester.

The year 1897 saw Queen Victoria's Diamond Jubilee, which was celebrated throughout the entire British Empire. Virtually every city, town and village was decorated for the occasion and, according to Albert

Bankes' diary on the 19th June he, 'drove on the top of a bus from Waterloo Station to Hyde Park Corner, Liverpool Street and back to Waterloo to see the Jubilee Decorations'. Jubilee Day was 22nd June when, 'At 11.15 am as the Queen left Buckingham Palace the sun came out and we had Queen's weather all day.'

Two days later and during the period 24th June to 17th July the announcements of the engagement and the forthcoming wedding of, 'Mr. Walter Bankes of Kingston Lacy and Corfe Castle and Miss Henrietta Fraser, Grandaughter of the late Mr. John Fraser JP of Brunchrew, Inverness and Mongewell Park', appeared in the *Court Journal, Daily Telegraph, Morning Post, Evening Standard, Whitehall Review, Hearth and Home* and *Sportsman*. The wordings of the announcements were all broadly similar, with the *Hearth and Home* taking up ten lines whereas the *Sportsman* simply stated that, 'The wedding of Mr. Ralph Bankes and Miss Fraser takes place in London on Wednesday next'.

The Wedding took place at Holy Trinity Church, Sloane Street, described in latter years by Sir John Betjeman as the 'Cathedral of the Arts and Craft Movement.' From an excellent guide book to the church by Peyton Skipwith, we learn that the building, which replaced an earlier and perfectly adequate one that was only fifty years old when it was demolished, was funded by Lord Cadogan who donated £20,000 (the equivalent of £1.5 million) plus the site. The cornerstone was laid by Beatrice, Countess Cadogan on Ascension Day, 30th May 1889. George Oakshott, the Churchwarden, whose name is inscribed on the stone as being one of those present, had in fact died the previous week, which, as is commented on in the Guide Book, goes to show that the best laid stones like the best laid plans. . . The Church was consecrated by the Bishop of London on 13th May 1890, just seven years before Henrietta's and Walter's wedding. One of the most striking features of this new church was, and still is, the great east window which was the largest ever made by Morris & Company.

It was, of course, a glamorous occasion with families of the bride and groom present together with representatives of most of the nobility local to Walter's Kingston Lacy and Corfe Castle Estate attending, and, taking place in a newly built church that represented all that was best in

Holy Trinity Church, Sloane Street (author)

the Arts and Craft Movement. The excitement of it all must have been intense, particularly for Henrietta.

Obviously it was not a 'Royal Wedding' nor was it a 'Society Wedding' but it would seem that it came into the category of a 'Fashionable Wedding'. We can get some indication of who came within this 'Fashionable' category by referring to the Marriage Supplement to the *Court Journal and Fashionable Gazette* for that period. Contained within the edition were brief details of 33 marriages of people who were deemed to come within the 'fashionable' category. Of the grooms there was one Honourable Gentleman, two Reverends, one Colonel, one Major, one Captain, two Doctors and twenty-five Mr's, one of whom was Mr. Walter Bankes.

Factual reports of the wedding appeared in the *Court Circular, Morning Post* and *Globe*. The *Court Journal* published two accounts. The first gave details of the wedding and the guests and was contained in ten column inches. The second, a much longer one of 25 inches, listed all the gifts, numbering something in the region of 400. As far as I can see there was no report in *The Times*.

The *Lady's Pictorial* also gave a detailed account of the occasion, in eleven column inches, listing the notable guests and presents together with two small photographs of the couple, although reference was made to the Fraser family home as being Monywell Park, not Mongewell Park.

Continuing the same theme of spelling mistakes the *North British Daily Mail* referred to Mr. John Fraser of Worgwell Park, Wallyford, and to Mr. Bankes of Corfe Castle and Kingston Lacey, Dorat. The *Liverpool Mercury* in giving a short but good account referred to Kingston Lacep.

The *Queen* devoted two column inches and rather nicely referred to 'the bride who was led to the Chancel Steps by her brother Mr. John Fraser'. The *Sportsman* announced that Miss Fraser got married to, 'that good sportsman, Mr. Ralph Bankes of Corfe Castle and Kingston Lacy.'

Locally the *Southern Times* of Weymouth devoted 25 column inches to their report whilst the *Dorset County Chronicle* also filled 25 inches and used the smallest type imaginable. The *Southern Guardian* and the *Bournemouth Guardian* each gave comprehensive coverage of the event and in its account, the *Bournemouth Observer* referred to the 'fashionable wedding'. The *Bridport News* headed its article, 'Sportsman's Wedding: A Dorset Gentleman leads his Bride to the Altar'.

Of the 'smart' magazines, Mrs. Papillon in *Vanity Fair* noted that 'there was a great deal of interest in the marriage of Miss Fraser, who is very handsome. She has made such a brilliant marriage.' In the October edition of *Lady's Realm* the writer observed that:

> . . . there were a great number of smart weddings taking place in Town quite late in the Season – very late indeed according to our reckoning of the Season, which each year seems to drag on further into the summer. One of these fashionable weddings was that of Mr. Ralph Bankes of Corfe Castle and Kingston Lacey to Miss Fraser, Grand Daughter of the late Mr. John Fraser of Brunchrew and Mongewell Park. Miss Fraser's was one of the white weddings which have been so much in vogue lately.

The last sentence is important.

The tradition of the white wedding dress with a veil became established during the 19th century, encouraged and probably influenced by the marriage of Queen Victoria, and later her children and her grand children. However white weddings were the preserve of the very wealthy, powerful families until the late 19th century and status could be measured in terms of fabric, lace, jewels and the number of bridesmaids, together with an impressive guest list, all reported in the pages of the *Queen* or the *Court Journal and Fashionable Gazette*. As we shall see Henrietta's wedding fulfilled all these criteria.

Mrs. Humphrey recorded in 1897:

> The white satin dress seems to be almost necessary to the legality of the Wedding ceremony, and it is worn by brides belonging to classes which can afford no opportunity for wearing of white satin except at the Wedding.

We can see from this, that whilst Henrietta probably could afford to wear satin on other occasions, and the Bankes and the Frasers were wealthy together with influence locally, they did not come into the category of being 'very wealthy and powerful'.

The marriage on Wednesday July 21st 1897 was solemnized by Rev. Eldon S. Bankes, Rector of Corfe Castle, supported by Rev. H. E. J. Bevan, Rector of Holy Trinity. The witnesses were Mr. John Fraser, Henrietta's brother, and Mr. Henry Weld Blundell who was the best man. On the marriage certificate Walter's age was given as 44 and Henrietta's as 29, and her residence at the time of the marriage as 7 Sloane Gardens. Perhaps one should not comment on a lady's age but as Henrietta was born in May 1867 and her wedding to Walter took place in July 1897 she was, shall we say, round about 29 years old.

The all important guest list for the wedding was headed by Prince and Princess Henry of Pless. He was a close friend of the Kaiser, and she was the former Mary Theresa Olivia Cornwallis-West, who was said a few years later to be one of the most beautiful women of her time and a brilliant member of Edwardian Society. They were followed in the guest list by two dukes and duchesses, nine earls and countesses and two viscounts and viscountesses, together with various members of their families. Lord and Lady Chelsea were also included, he being the eldest son of Lord Cadogan and she being Mildred Cecilia Harriet née Sturt, the third daughter of Lord and Lady Alington of Crichel. There followed representatives from almost all the local titled families and among the untitled were Mr. and Mrs. Alexander Casper Fraser together with various other members of the Fraser family. Mr. and Mrs. Albert Bankes were also invited and from his diary he tells us that he was a 'pew opener'. There were, as a number of the newspaper reports stated, 'many other guests.'

Henrietta wore a dress of white satin veiled in white *mousseline de soie* with a long Court train falling from the shoulders, tulle veil and wreath of natural orange blossoms, and she was attended by eight bridesmaids of whom Miss Jessy Fraser was the chief bridesmaid. They were attired in costumes of white tulle over white satin, trimmed with guipure lace and sashes of turquoise blue silk; white chiffon hats with plumes of white ostrich feathers and blue ribbons. The bridegroom's presents to them were bouquets of pink roses and diamond and enamel brooches. At the conclusion of the ceremony, the bridal party drove to the town house of the bride's brother, Mr. John Fraser, in Wilton Crescent where the wedding reception was held, and later in the afternoon the newly married couple left town for Folkestone, en route for the continent. Henrietta's travelling dress was of fawn coloured poplin, with white chiffon hat, trimmed with forget-me-nots.

There were about 400 wedding presents, including many costly gifts of jewellery and plate. Walter's Dorset and Wiltshire tenants sent a handsome piece of plate, accompanied by an illuminated address, bound in morocco, containing the names of some 600 subscribers. The inhabitants of Wimborne contributed a piece of plate and an address, these were to be presented, together with the tenants' gift, on the homecoming of the bride and groom on the 21st August, when a garden party was planned for the occasion at Kingston Lacy.

4
Henrietta's Homecoming

T HE ARRIVAL of the happy couple home from their honeymoon was pleasantly reported in the *Bournemouth Guardian* dated Saturday 21st August and is paraphrased here:

> HOME-COMING OF MR. AND MRS. BANKES. Mr. W. R. Bankes, the owner of The Corfe Castle and Kingston Lacy Estate, brought his bride home to Kingston Lacy House on Tuesday evening, and met with an enthusiastic reception. The Minster bells pealed out as Mr. and Mrs. Bankes were driven through Wimborne from the railway station, and there was a display of bunting at houses along the route from the town to Kingston Lacy. At Hillbutts, opposite the residence of Mr. Lodder (one of the stewards of the estate), a very fine triple arch had been erected, the design being that of an old castle covered with holly. There was a large concourse of people in waiting to give Mr. and Mrs. Bankes a cordial welcome, and Messrs. Chislett and Lodder (the estate stewards) were to

Celebration arch, Hillbutts, 1897 (National Trust)

the fore with congratulations. The horses were removed from the carriage, which was then drawn to the mansion – a distance of about a mile – by a number of willing men, who were afterwards entertained to a substantial repast. A second triumphal arch was passed near the entrance to the park. Mr. and Mrs. Bankes repeatedly acknowledged the salutations of the crowd and Mr. Bankes expressed his thanks for such a kindly welcome home.

It would appear that the building of 'triumphal' arches was the usual practice on estates when the local landowner returned home with his bride, as we shall see later when Henrietta's sister is married.

Two little gems of researched history that have come to light are drafts of a letter written by Henrietta to her brother John just after her arrival at Kingston Lacy. What a happy bride she sounds, thoroughly enjoying the welcome from the tenants but still mindful of the cost of the entire wedding, which she had to bear, and very conscience of the dignity expected of her in her new role as mistress of Kingston Lacy.

I received your letter late last night, you must please remember that I am in the wilds of the country, and only two posts a day, one now at 12.00 noon and one at six in the afternoon.

We arrived here yesterday afternoon and received a perfect ovation – the whole town and village turned out, and the station was packed with people. There were two splendid arches erected, great big ones, of holly and green stuff, and the horses were taken out of the carriage and we were pulled along by fifty men right up to the house, a good one and a half miles, all cheering and shouting. It was really great fun.

Ralph had ordered a very fine pair of gee-gees and the whole thing went off in grand style. The whole route was be-bannered and be-flagged and I said that the two arches were to be left up till after Monday, as you and Jess must see them so do make an effort to come on Monday by the 2.25 train.

I grinned all the time yesterday driving along as I had to go a bobbing all the way just like the old Queen did, and all the people curtseying and scraping, great joke!!

Garden Party, 1897 (National Trust)

Saturday is going to be a most tremendous business, over 1100 have accepted, and great preparations in the Park and Garden. Heaps and heaps of tables and stands, and platforms for bands. All for ME.

There are going to be two presentations and addresses to Ralph and me and we are to stand on the big balcony to receive them.

You and Jess had better order what you think is necessary, but please do not be too extravagant and reckless, as you know after all this wedding business, what enormous bills I have to pay, as not a thing is paid for yet, and all, every scrap, has to come out of my pocket. But tell Jess while she is about it, not to stint on a 5/- or 10/- but get what is necessary and neat. I thought she had plenty of underwear and chemises as I gave her six of mine only last May, and they were in a very good state.

I am quite sick with longing to see you and my little lamb. For five weeks I hav'nt seen any of my very own – I am dreading the Garden Party.

I want to impress strongly on you, when we meet at the station not to be too demonstrative, remember I am the object of every eye and mind.

Damn it.

Ever yours

J. B.

But as was mentioned earlier the celebrations did not end there, and a paraphrased account by the *Western Gazette* dated 27 August 1897 is presented here:

On Saturday 21st August Mr. and Mrs. W. Ralph Bankes entertained over a thousand guests at a garden party at Kingston Lacy the company comprising gentry of the neighbourhood, tenantry on the Corfe Castle and Kingston Lacy Estates and representatives of the town and trade of Wimborne. For the convenience of those tenants coming from Corfe Castle, Studland and Swanage, Mr. Bankes had kindly arranged for a special train which left Swanage at half past one and arrived at Wimborne Station at half past two. Brakes and waggonettes were in waiting to convey this party to Kingston Lacy and the drive was much enjoyed. The scene on the road was an animated one there being an almost continuous stream of all sorts and conditions of conveyances from the smart landau and pair down to the humble donkey cart with 'Neddy' gaily rosetted for the occasion . . . plentiful display of bunting on houses along the route . . . the arch still standing at Hillbutts and at the entrance lodge . . .

. . . Arrangements admirably made under the direct super-intendence of Mr. T. Lodder. . . The weather delightfully fine . . . the tea tents being only needed for storage . . . temporary bandstands erected for the Wimborne Town Band and the Poole Rifle Volunteer Band.

Mr. and Mrs. Bankes received their numerous guests at the approach to the terrace and gave each a cordial welcome. Mrs. Bankes, whose charm of manner made a most happy impression on all, wore a pale blue spotted muslin gown trimmed with cream lace, and her white toque had trimmings of forget-me-nots and white ostrich plumes . . . tea was taken on long rows of tables in front of the terrace, about eleven hundred persons being present . . . guests congregated around the terrace steps where Mr. Chisslett called for order and the interesting function of presenting Mr. Bankes with the wedding presents then took place.

First present came from the tenancy. Three handsome silver bowls in the pattern of Charles II, the largest one being inscribed. The accompanying address was beautifully bound in book form. Mr. T. D. Joyce whose family have been tenants for three generations made the presentation . . . beginning of a new era in the history of the estate. To the many valuable pocessions in Kingston Lacy House, Mr. Bankes had added a far more costly and precious jewel to add to the adornments. (Cheers)

Mr. Bankes said he hardly knew where to begin to thank them for their kindness in coming there, for the splendid address . . . a perfect work of art and the gifts . . . that Dame Fortune never came to a man with both hands full, on one hand these beautiful presents, and on the other, indicating Mrs. Bankes, something more beautiful to show them, (Cheers)

The gift of the Townspeople of Wimborne, a handsome silver salver, richly chased, was next brought forward. This was supplied by Mr. Hapgood, Jeweller. An illuminated framed address accompanied the gift and bore views of Kingston Lacy House, Corfe Castle ruins, Wimborne Minster and the Grammar School. Dr. Parkinson in making the presentation said the people of Wimborne could not let this auspicious event go by without marking it with some expression of their feeling of pleasure . . . he also expressed regret at losing from among them Miss Bankes (Walter's sister) who had been such a kind friend to the poor in the district. He assured Miss Bankes that she would carry away with her the esteem of all . . . the blessing that attended those who considered the poor and needy.

Mr. Bankes thanked them again and particularly for the reference to his sister. The health of Mr. and Mrs. Bankes was afterwards drunk with much enthusiasm. Following the presentations, dancing and other amusements took place and the celebrations closed at 7.00 o'clock with the combined bands playing God Save the Queen. The train for Corfe Castle and Swanage left Wimborne at 8.00pm.

Henrietta and Walter attended the Morning Service at the Minster on the following Sunday and at the close of the Service the organist played a Wedding March and the Minster bells were rung.

The *Sunday Times* dated August 22nd 1897 also reported the event in one paragraph: 'Mr. and Mrs. Bankes gave a garden party this week to the neighbourhood at Kingston Lacy – we suppose to introduce Mrs. Bankes to the county on her recent marriage.'

5
The Family Years

AFTER ALL THE EXCITEMENT of 1897 Henrietta probably set about the business of family life and organising the running of the house and possibly Walter.

The 23rd June 1898 saw the birth of their first child, Daphne Adelaide. Whether the firstborn, a girl, and not a 'son and heir' was a disappointment to Henrietta and Walter is difficult to judge. Walter's reaction is open to conjecture but it would appear there was no public announcement of the birth. Albert Bankes in his diary wrote in one line, 'Jennie Bankes had a little girl. I am very sorry it was not a boy'.

By now the pattern of hosting social events for the local people whether they were tenants of the Estate or not was being established; they usually took place at Christmas and in August. Albert Bankes tells us that during August 1898 the 'Kingston Lacy Lawn Tennis Club held its Party and there were about 105 people present'. Christmas 1898 saw a hundred children from Pamphill being entertained to tea at the Mansion. 'After justice had been done to the good things provided, presents were distributed from the Christmas Tree, Mr. and Mrs. Bankes being assisted by Miss Fraser'.

However not all Dorset children were enjoying themselves as Beryl, Lady Digby records in her Diary for December 1898: 'Diphtheria in several cottages at Little Minterne and Lyons Gate. National School shut in consequence.'

It was in 1899 that Henrietta inaugurated the Kingston Lacy Cottage Garden Competition to encourage cottagers on the Estate to improve the management and cultivation of their gardens. Over the Christmas period of that year 280 children were entertained at the House. They were taken there in vehicles supplied by the local farmers and all the children received presents. Additionally on another occasion about one hundred employees together with their wives and children were entertained, the children receiving presents, and the head of the household a plum pudding.

Viola Florence Geraldine was born on 11th February 1900. Here again we are led to believe that Henrietta and Walter were disappointed that the new arrival was not a 'Son and Heir.' No mention was made of the birth in Albert Bankes diary. By this time Henrietta was only four months short of her thirty-third birthday and she may well have wondered if time was running out for her to give birth to a son, so very important to this level of society at that time.

August 1900 and Albert Bankes, via his diary, tells us of the Kingston Lacy Garden Party with about 120 guests, including Jessie and Jack Fraser, Henrietta's sister and brother, together with Edmund Fraser, a Diplomat late of Pretoria, he being a distant cousin of Henrietta.

On 22nd January 1901 Queen Victoria died, Out went the Victorian era and in came the Edwardian era in the ample shape of King Edward VII.

A paragraph in the *Week End* dated 31st August 1901 perhaps gives us a glimpse of life at Kingston Lacy.

> With so lovely a home, it is little wonder that Mrs. Bankes prefers to entertain a constant succession of house parties, to prolonged stays in her charming town house. London consequently does not see very much of either Mr. Bankes or his pretty wife.

The annual Kingston Lacy Garden Party took place on 13th August and Albert Bankes' diary records that, 'The Infanta Eulalie of Spain came over from Brownsea Island with the Van Raaltes'. A further entry, dated 30th September 1901, in Albert Bankes' diary tells us that:

> Ralph and Jennie had an accident with their motor yesterday near White Mill colliding with a tradesman's van. Ralph says he cannot stop his motor dead which sounds dangerous.

White Mill, c.1898 (National Trust)

In the 1901 census return for Kingston Lacy Park, Walter R. Bankes is recorded as the 'Head, Married, age 47, Living on own means' and born in 'Shapwick, Dorset'. However for his wife, Henrietta J. Bankes it is recorded that she is aged 30 and born in London, Paddington.

The following year, 1902, was to be eventful for the Nation as well as for Henrietta and Walter. In February, Walter's cousin, Gladys, daughter of Florrie and Albert Bankes married, in Charminster Church, Sir Hugh Nicholas Granville Stucley who later became a Baronet.

It would seem that the summer of that year was rather late in arriving, as commented on by the *Daily Express* dated June 13th when it refered to a:

> Roseless June. Poor supply of seasonable fruit and flowers. June sulked again yesterday, while winter still lingers on. Under a dull leaden sky that dripped rain frequently with chilled pedestrians hurrying through sloppy streets, London's aspect was that of a bleak and melancholy November day. No one is having heat rash, chilblains are rampant and sunstroke has given way to lumbago and sciatica.

However everyone was looking forward to the Coronation of King Edward VII and Queen Alexandra on June 26th, but even that proved to be a dreadful disappointment when the King was taken ill with appendicitis shortly before the appointed day. The Ceremony was postponed, and most of the visiting Royalty and other dignitaries from around the world decided to return home.

Henrietta and Walter had other things on their mind as their third child was due in early July. Then, at last, on Monday 14th at 34 Wilton Crescent, London, Henry John Ralph, the 'Son and Heir' was born.

Purchasers of the *Bournemouth Daily Echo* on that Monday would have read of the resignation of the Marquess of Salisbury (The Prime Minister) and Mr. Balfour to be his successor, and there were rumours of a General Election. There were 'Hints to ladies. How to dress and what to do' and on the sports pages details of C. B. Fry's 78 not out for Sussex against Surrey. There was an advertisement giving details of the sale of 75 Bus Horses at the stables in Pokesdown and an advert for Mitcham Cricket Green Cigarettes.

However it was not until Wednesday July 16th that the same newspaper told it's readers that there were:

REJOICINGS AT KINGSTON LACEY [*sic*] AND CORFE CASTLE. The Wimborne Minster bells were rung yesterday in honour of the birth on Monday at 34 Wilton Crescent SW of a son and heir to Mr. and Mrs. W. Ralph Bankes of Kingston Lacey [*sic*] and Corfe Castle.

The following Saturday, the 19th, the *Bournemouth Guardian*, announced, under the heading, Wimborne:

A SON AND HEIR – The owner of the Kingston Lacey [*sic*] and Corfe Castle Estates (Mr. W. R. Bankes) has been presented with a son and heir. The Minster bells were rung on Tuesday in honour of the event.

The above statement was confined to five lines whereas, under the same Wimborne heading details of an 'Accident to a cricketer' took up 13 lines and 'Servant in trouble' 22 lines.

Throughout the entire Estate there must have been a considerable sense of relief that at last a son had arrived to carry on the long line of the Bankes of Kingston Lacy.

Amongst all the celebrations the one at Corfe Castle was probably fairly typical and possibly the noisiest. The *Western Gazette* dated 18th July 1902 announced that there was:

Great Rejoicing – As Mr. Bankes of Kingston Lacy House is Lord of the Manor of Corfe Castle, owner of the Castle and much property in this place, great rejoicing took place on Tuesday when it was made known by Telegram, that a son and heir had been born to him . . . Mr. William Wiseman, the Custodian of the castle had flags flying and bunting displayed at the gateway. Mr. Thomas Luther and others also had flags waving in the breeze. Cannon was fired at intervals while the bells rang merrily and in the evening the band went up into the Castle under Bandmaster Stockley and played appropriate selections to which some danced. That the young heir may grow up to be healthy, a pride to his parents and a blessing to his tenants and a God fearing man is the heartfelt wish of all in Corfe Castle. Best Wishes and congratulations to the Lord of the Manor and Mrs. Bankes.

The Christening of the 'Son and Heir' took place on Tuesday 23rd of September 1902. Albert Bankes, in his Diary noted that:

> We went in four carriages to Wimborne Minster to the Christening by the Rev. Huish of Henry John Ralph Bankes of Kingston Lacy. The Bells rang many peels and the organ played. I was never asked to do so but as there did not appear to be any God Parents or proxies about I answered for them just to prevent a pause.

The *Wimborne Minster Parish Magazine* for October 1902 recorded a number of Baptisms including, on September 5th, Janet Edith, daughter of Frederick William and Lucy Richards, and on the 23rd Henry John Ralph Bankes, son of Walter and Jenny Henriette [*sic*] Bankes. On another page under the heading Colehill we learn that:

> This district is rapidly increasing in numbers and importance. Our beautiful little Chapel of Ease, St. Michael and All Angels, is doing good work and is well attended; but a serious inconvenience is the absence of any resident clergyman . . . Mr. Bankes has made a most welcome and generous gift to the district of an acre of ground close to the Church whereon a house for a clergyman may be built . . . Sincere thanks . . .

Christmas 1902 must have been a wonderfully happy time for Henrietta, her family and probably the whole household, as it was the 'son and heir's' first Christmas. The *Western Gazette* records that there were, at Kingston Lacy:

> FESTIVE GATHERINGS – Mr. and Mrs. Bankes recently entertained the employees of the Kingston Lacy Estate together with their wives to a substantial tea. On leaving the men were supplied with plum puddings.
>
> On New Years Eve children over seven attending the Pamphill, Shapwick and Holt Schools were invited to a tea and entertainment at the house. Messrs. Cave, Tory, Kent, James, Coombes and Bendall kindly conveyed the children to the house in wagons.

On New Years Day the inmates of the Almshouses and the women of St. Margaret's Hospital were entertained to dinner at the mansion to which they were driven in carriages from the house. At the various gatherings Mrs. Bankes studied in every way the comfort and happiness of her guests.

For the spring of 1903 Albert Bankes' diary tells us that he lunched with:

Ralph and Jennie at their new house 'The Knoll' in Studland. A most delightful house for a really hot summer as it is built in a middle of a clump of fir trees on a slight mound. No garden round it so there is nothing to keep up or tidy.

During the summer of that year the inmates of the Almshouses (St. Margarets) in Wimborne together with the Union Workhouse were entertained by Mr. and Mrs. Bankes. About 100 people enjoyed tea on the lawn together with games, and 'before separating' each man was given 2oz of tobacco and the women tea, the children receiving sweets. These were the children from the Workhouse! The guests were conveyed to the house by brakes, presumably provided by the house. A (possible) misprint from one report tells us that the men received 2ozs of tobacco and the women ten!

On the 23rd October the *Dorset County Chronicle* gave details of the:

COTTAGE GARDEN COMPETITION – The Cottage Garden Competition, inaugurated by Mrs. Bankes has been again the means of producing some excellent work in the management and cultivation of gardens attached to the cottages of this district. The Committee met about 40 cottagers and gave details of the Competition since its establishment in 1899. The Committee for inspection are Messrs. J. P. Chissell, F. W. Richards and T. Lodder. . . two first prizes of £ 1 each to J. Galpin and H. Scott.

That represented about £60 in present day values.

But 1903 closed with concern over Walter's Health.

6
Walter's Failing Health

THE FIRST the wider public knew of Walter's ill health was when the *Southern Echo* dated 31st October 1903 announced:

ILLNESS OF MR. RALPH BANKES We regret to announce the illness of Mr. W. Ralph Bankes the owner of Corfe Castle and other property. He was staying at Studland but on becoming ill he went to Kingston Lacy, Wimborne where he is being medically attended. It is understood that Mr. Bankes is suffering from heart trouble. On enquiring our representative was informed that an improvement of conditions had taken place.

Albert had been told of the situation by Henrietta a few days earlier and from then on the local Press recorded Walter's deteriorating health assiduously.

The usual Christmas and New Year's festivities have this year been somewhat curtailed by reason of Mr. Bankes' illness. However the now usual rounds of teas, lunches and parties for all the locals, young and old, together with plum puddings being given and in the case of the Shapwick poor, 4 cwt. of coal each. The reader will be pleased to learn that Mr. Bankes is making slow but satisfactory progress towards recovery.

During January 1904 Albert visited Kingston Lacy and, '. . . found poor Ralph very weak and breathing with difficulty', but in March they were able to have lunch together at the Boscombe Hotel when Walter was, '. . . very much better and regaining health.'

In April Walter's health continued in a volatile state. On one occasion Albert Bankes when visiting Kingston Lacy found him, 'looking very ill and weak', and later during the day Albert, 'walked to Wimborne with Jessie Fraser and gave her tea at Gush's confectionery shop.'

Later in the month Henrietta and Walter visited their house, 'The Knoll' in Studland and during this time Walter was able to, 'drive in his pony carriage to see his new Alms Houses'.

During May the *Dorset County Chronicle* reported that:

> . . . we regret to hear that the condition of Mr. Bankes who is still at Studland, shows no improvement. Mr. Bankes returned to Kingston Lacy House on Saturday. He bore the journey as well as could be expected, but his condition is still serious.'

Albert noted that, 'he is now very delirious and weak'.

For the *Bournemouth Graphic*, dated 2nd June 1904 the news of Walter's illness appeared to be a mere preamble to more interesting items. However under the heading 'Entre Nous' sorrow was expressed on hearing that:

> . . . Mr. Bankes, of Kingston Lacy, is lying seriously ill at his residence. He is being attended by Mr. T. B. Scott, whose motor-car runs there and back during the week mounting up to a total of about 170 miles. Mr. Bankes is well known as the possessor of most beautiful and valuable pictures, including a Romney portrait, which is, I believe, valued at £20,000 [*£1.25m at current values*].

The materialistic world was apparently very much alive and well!

A few days later, the same newspaper in their 'Notes from Swanage' observed that:

> The Studland people have made quite a big hit with their steam ferry arrangements, and it bids fair to make the place look up. They are enlarging their borders by building, and Mr. Bankes who owns nearly the whole of Studland, has built a reading room among the trees, with an almshouse at each end.

Albert, on one of his regular visits to London, travelled to Waterloo Station, 'in the new corridor train which is most comfortable.'

During late July HRH King Edward VII visited Mr. and Mrs. George Cavendish-Bentinck at Highcliffe Castle. The house party who met His Majesty was a small one and included Lord and Lady Alington, and it was on this occasion that an invitation was conveyed to His Majesty to be their guest at Crichel during the following year.

By September Walter appeared to be 'holding his own' although Albert observed that he, Walter, was 'decidedly better and in his bath chair on the lawn.'

Meanwhile life on the Estate continued. A new wing, consisting of a smoking room and cloak room with a bedroom over, was added to Pamphill Manor, and for the rest of society the *Bournemouth Graphic* offered some useful information telling their readers how to make use of their leisure time.

> Where to go for Blackberries? The blackberrying season is now with us, and everywhere this year there seems to be a profusion of this delightful fruit. And perhaps there is no form of amusement more productive of merriment and keen pleasure for young people than blackberrying picnics.

Sadly times have changed!

By now Walter's bed had been placed in the Library in Kingston Lacy House providing him access to books and documents which occupied his mind and helped to pass the long hours From here he was able to easily be moved out on to the South Terrace.

The mood at Kingston Lacy throughout the summer must have been one of resignation amongst the family and staff and generally a feeling of helplessness, not knowing what to do or say for the best, and for Henrietta in particular, a fear for what the future would bring. Walter, the man of action, the sportsman (plus his reputation for 'wine, women and song') confined to his bed or at best an armchair, what were his thoughts? Did the frustration of it all burst out in bouts of bad temper and impatience? The National Trust guidebook to Kingston Lacy tells us that Walter was 'communicating with the servants mainly through written notes' but we must remember that, unlike today, there was little a Doctor could do to ease the symptoms of someone suffering heart disease, which makes the difficulties that Walter was probably having in his relationships with other people very understandable.

In her book *Why Not?*, Viola Bankes observed:

> . . . for a man of such beguiling charm and courtesy it must be admitted that the moods towards the end of his life became strangely difficult . . . A year or so before he died he was compelled to give up shooting, racing and yachting on account of his heart. . . One of the finest sportsman on the continent and in England spent the last months that remained to him sunk in an arm chair too ill to walk. . . Soon he was unable to leave his bed. . .

Walter died, aged 51, at 10.30 am on Sunday 20th November 1904.

Although Walter had been ill for over a year the news of his death may well have come as a shock to his uncle, Albert Bankes. His diary entry for that date tells us that:

> At 5.00 pm a special messenger bought me a letter from Dorchester Station to say that dear Ralph died quite quietly and suddenly. He was feeling so well that Jennie went upstairs to get ready for Church and he got out of bed to get a deed he wanted. The exertion was too great for his heart which stopped and it was all over. The nurse rushed up and told Jennie who could not believe it having left him fairly well only a few minutes previously.

Mr. Lodder, the Agent was at the Minster at the time, and his being called from the church led many to believe that Mr. Bankes had passed away. The tolling of the bell after the service confirmed this. The Minster rang muffled peals before the evening service, and at the conclusion of the service. Mr. A. E. Wilshire played the 'Dead March' from *Saul*, during which the whole of the congregation remained standing.

The following day Albert travelled by train from Dorchester and,

> Reached Kingston Lacy at 9.30 am and found poor Jennie quite dazed. I saw poor Ralph in his bed in the Library. I had my luggage with me but as

Jennie was too dazed to say whether she wanted me to stay or not I returned home by the 4.30 train.

How much Henrietta was aware of the details of Walter's Will is unclear but it would seem that as far as the codicil dated 6th April 1903 was concerned she was totally unaware of its existence. Tradition has it that county families as well as those in more elevated circumstances buried their dead alongside their ancestors in either the family vault or in their local churchyard. Walter's codicil defied this tradition by stating that he was to be cremated and only his ashes were to be interned in the family vault in Wimborne Minster. In it Walter stated that:

> I desire that after my decease my body be cremated at the Woking Crematorium in accordance with the customary rites of the Church of England that the ashes be placed in a gold urn to be supplied by Messieurs Elkington and sealed by them that the urn be then taken to Kingston Lacy and afterwards by and with the consent of the Wimborne Church Governors and any other necessary Authority be placed in the Bankes Family Vault in Wimborne Minster and that a funeral service be held at Studland Church simultaneously with that of the Cremation which shall be as short as possible by the Reverend Frederick Swift Algeo the Rector and I give to the said Frederick Swift Algeo the sum of one hundred pounds for his trouble in holding such service.

The coffin of polished oak was removed from Kingston Lacy in the morning of Thursday 24th November 1904 and a memorial service was held in the Minster. The cortège left the mansion at nine o'clock and included, besides relatives, the employees on the estate and several of the oldest tenants, Messrs. H.W.Cave, E.W.Cave, J.P.Chissell, W.D.Kent, Percy Tory, George Arthur, Fred Richards and Tom Joyce, acting as pall-bearers. The cortege was met at the entrance to West Street by a force of Police from Wimborne and the sub-divisions of Cranborne and Branksome, under Supt. Marsh, then proceeded through the Square to the Minster. Within the Minster a large congregation had assembled, including clergy, representatives of the county families, the magistrates, the Minster and School Governors, members of the Wimborne Urban District Council, tradesmen, tenants from all parts of the deceased's extensive estates, and inhabitants of Wimborne and district. Additionally several of the coastguards from Studland Bay in uniform were also present under Chief Officer J. Pride.

As the congregation was assembling the organist played Chopin's 'Funeral March' and 'O Rest in the Lord.' On the arrival of the cortège at the Minster it was met at the north door by the clergy and a full choir, and the coffin, upon which was a magnificent cross of violets from Henrietta together with beautiful little wreaths from the young daughters, Daphne and Viola, and the son and heir, Henry John Ralph who by now was two years and four months old. The 89th Psalm was chanted to *Felton*, and the hymns sung were 'Lead kindly light' and 'Brief life is here our portion.' The opening sentences were said by the Rev. Canon Sowter, and the rest of the Service was taken by the Rev. Canon Bankes who only seven years previously had conducted Henrietta's and Walter's wedding ceremony. The other clergy present were the Revs. Canon Hart-Dyke, C.H.Gould and M.K.Exham. As the congregation were leaving the building Beethoven's 'Funeral March' was played.

After the service the remains were conveyed by the 11.40 train from Wimborne Station to the crematorium at St. John's, Woking, where the committal prayers were said, and where Walter's body was cremated as instructed. Simultaneously a memorial service was held in the Parish Church at Studland.

Albert Bankes final remark sums up the sorrow and stress imposed upon the family and in particular Henrietta, with extra travelling and a longer drawn out burial when he wrote in his diary this final paragraph on the day's events:

> I think if people only realized how distasteful cremation is to the sorrowing relations they would never leave in their wills the wish to be cremated. Poor Jennie, I know was horrified at the idea but we dare not set aside poor Ralph's instruction.

It must have been a very long and distressing day for Henrietta.

7
Life After Walter

Announcements of Walter's death appeared in the *Times, Daily Telegraph, the Standard, Evening News, Post, Star, Morning Leader, Advertiser* and *Madras Mail.*

Most of them noted that, 'he was a typical country gentleman, a fine shot and a good judge of horses'.

The *Times* gave, probably the best write up highlighting his interest in art and that he placed, 'many of his fine pictures at the disposal of the Royal Academy. All his best pictures have been seen in London due to his kindness.'

Walter died a month before Christmas 1904 and for any family with young children it would normally be a time of eager anticipation of the coming festive season. How close Daphne, who was six years old at the time of Walter's death, Viola four and Ralph two were to their father is difficult to judge but at that level of society they would have spent more time in the company of their governess than their parents. Any enquiry, although unlikely, by the children to the servants relating to the whereabouts of their father, may have put the servants in a very difficult situation; it would not have been for them to explain the full circumstances of their father's absence and the air of gloom pervading the house.

Perhaps Henrietta did explain to her children what had happened to their father but, if due to Walter's ill health they had seldom seen him during the previous year or so, and therefore were unable to relate to any one particular person, the full significance of what she was telling them failed to register in their minds. Hence the popular belief that the news of Walter's death and all its implications was withheld from them. In the minds of children of that age whatever their status, the eager anticipation of Christmas would have been paramount, and life for everyone including the tenants and cottagers had to get back to some semblance of normality, 'for the sake of the children at Christmas'.

The *Dorset County Chronicle* dated 22nd December 1904 records:

PAMPHILL SCHOOL PRIZE GIVING: There was a good attendance of parents and friends at the prize giving which took place in the schoolroom last Tuesday . . . Busy hands had been at work the previous day in decorating the room . . . brightened and almost transformed in appearance. . . much credit to those who undertook the task.

Twice during the year had the school come out at the head of the list in the quarterly returns for average attendance . . . obtained a fame of which others might be proud . . . remembering that many of the little ones have to walk some distance, some, three miles in inclement weather . . . Mrs. Bankes took such a kindly interest in the school . . . had distributed the prizes last year and in her deep sorrow had not forgotten them this year and had sent prizes.

The *Western Gazette* also noted: 'The prizes were gracefully distributed by Mrs. Fletcher who made a charming speech.' The article concluded by stating: 'Each child was presented with a bun and an orange by Sir John and Lady Hanham and before separating gave hearty cheers for all who had taken part in the proceedings.'

Probate was granted in February 1905. Obviously Henrietta and the children were remembered with more than adequate secure financial provisions but Walter had also remembered some members of the Estate whose loyalty he appreciated. Mr. Crook, coachman and Mr. Hoare, gamekeeper were each presented with bequests of £250 (approximately the equivalent of £16,000 in present days values), Mr. Lodder, the Agent, receiving £2,000 (approximate equivalent £125,000). The Little Sisters of the Poor were remembered with a gift of £2,000 and the Church Lad's Brigade, £1,000.

By far the largest bequest was given to Elisabeth Marshall who, it was said, was Walter's mistress. The gift to her took the form of £40,000 in cash plus the freehold of two properties in Studland, namely Knoll House and Coombe House. Some time later Henrietta bought the properties back at considerable expense. However the most enduring symbol to come from Walter's will is St. Stephen's Church, Pamphill. The bequest was: '. . . to my Trustees a sum of five thousand pounds for the purpose of building and endowing or contributing towards building and endowing a Church at Pamphill, Dorset'.

Henrietta and the Trustees lost no time in fulfilling his instructions and we learn from Albert Bankes' diary that on the 13th February he,'. . . arrived at Kingston Lacy to see, with Jennie (Henrietta) the site of the new Church'; and the following day Henrietta, Albert and Mr. Lodder oversaw the pegging out of the site.

It was not until March 29th 1905 that Walter's ashes were finally laid to rest in the Family Vault in the Crypt at Wimborne Minster. The previous day Jerome Bankes arrived at Albert Bankes' home, Wolfeton House with the gold vase containing Walter's ashes, this, Albert 'locked up for the night in the wine cellar for safety sake.'

The following day Albert travelled: 'By 7.15 train with Jerome and the casket to Wimborne where we found Jennie in her carriage and drove with her to Wimborne Minster.' The Crypt was quite ready and open and after a short service Walter's ashes were placed in the family vault.

There is no doubt that Henrietta was held in high esteem locally and she was invited to lay the Foundation Stone of the new Church House, Wimborne Minster on Wednesday 13th September. The stone can still be seen to the right of the main entrance on the corner of the building at pavement level.

The latter part of 1905 was, for Henrietta, to be a very eventful few months, starting with the marriage, on the 26th October, of her sister, Jessie Maud to Sir Bourchier Wrey, owner of the Tawstock Court Estate near Barnstaple, North Devon. As we have seen, Henrietta married a man some fourteen years older than herself but Jessie's husband was some twenty-five years older than his bride, Jessie being twenty-five when they were married.

The *North Devon Journal's* very detailed report of the occasion gives us a glimpse into a bygone age:

> There was a large and fashionable assembly on Thursday afternoon at St. Paul's Church, Knightsbridge, London, SW, to witness the marriage of Sir Bourchier Wrey, 11th Bart, (creation 1628), J.P. for Devonshire, of Tawstock Court, Barnstaple, North Devon and Miss Jessie Maud Fraser, daughter of the late Mr. W. T. Fraser, and granddaughter of the late Mr. John Fraser, of Mongewell Park, Oxon.
>
> The church was handsomely decorated with tall Vienna palms, banked with white lilies and chrysanthemums and the altar vases were specially refilled with white flowers for the occasion. The nuptial ceremony was impressively conducted by the Rev. Albany B. S. Wrey (brother of the bridegroom) assisted by the Rev. Montagu Villiers, Prebendary of St. Paul's Cathedral and the Rev. J. Baden Powell, Precentor of St. Paul's Church.
>
> The bride was accompanied by her uncle, Mr. Arthur Fraser of Mongewell Park . . .   There were neither bridesmaids nor pages . . .   The reception held by Mrs. Bankes, of Kingston Lacy, sister of the bride. . .

The reporting of the couple's arrival home was no less detailed:

> A unique honour awaited Sir Bourchier and Lady Wrey on their arrival at Barnstaple Junction Station yesterday by the 3.50 p.m. down train for whilst detonators were fired and the church bells rang and Lady Wrey was presented by Miss Copp of Sticklepath, with an exquisite bouquet, Sir Bourchier Wrey's squadron of the Royal North Devon Hussars paraded 72 strong and formed a travelling escort through Lake village to Tawstock Court. . .

The decorations at Tawstock and its hamlets were on an extensive scale. No fewer than five triumphal arches were created in different parts of the parish, the structures (in the construction of which evergreens and flags and banners were employed) being no less artistic than they were imposing'.

The year 1905 would end with a Royal occasion and it was on Thursday December 7th that HRH King Edward VII visited Kingston Lacy.

8

A Royal Visitor

A S PREVIOUSLY STATED, the invitation to visit the Crichel Estate for a few days was conveyed to His Majesty King Edward VII on the occasion of his weekend visit to Highcliffe Castle, Christchurch, when he was the guest of Mr. and Mrs. George Cavendish-Bentinck, Lord and Lady Alington also being guests at the small house party which took place during July 1904. The invitation to visit Crichel was accepted by His Majesty and it took place early in December 1905.

Prior to the event the *Pall Mall Gazette* informed their readers that:

> Kingston Lacy, which the King is to visit during his sojourn in Dorsetshire, is a fine old place. . . Inigo Jones had something to do with it's designs . . . attraction being the Spanish Room with its walls covered (like Miles Standish's legs) with Cordova leather.

When Henrietta heard of the planned visit of His Majesty to Kingston Lacy considerable preparations were put in hand. Viola, in her book *Why Not?* records that the impending visit filled her, 'with apprehension and excitement', and this was probably a fair description of the atmosphere throughout the entire Household.

It would seem that Henrietta quickly turned for some guidance to 'Uncle' Albert Bankes, who, moving around on the fringes of high society, was well versed in the etiquette of the time. Henrietta may well not have had the experience of entertaining this level of society where the slightest

social gaff would be the talk of the chattering classes and no-one would
ever be allowed to forget it.

In his reply to a letter from Henrietta, Albert offered some useful
guidance and help on the day:

> I think the Panelled Dining Room is an excellent idea with the big round
> table in centre with white cloth on, either silver candelabra with candles
> or vase of flowers in centre. Table to be covered with plates of bread
> and cakes but chairs only to be placed on the organ side so that no one
> sits back to King. . . After planting the Tree all the party could leave
> their wraps in the Library, then go straight to the Spanish Room, Saloon
> and Drawing Room and finish by going into the Panelled Dining Room
> to tea.

His letter continued with helpful advice on such items as the seating
arrangements for the guests, together with some other suggestions to
ensure that the whole occasion went smoothly:

> On the sideboard you might have a bottle of whisky, siphons of soda and
> a bottle of Claret and Port in case any of the Gentlemen don't drink tea.
> This would look simply as if the wine was left there as usual for your own
> use and I could ask the Gentlemen whether they preferred whisky to tea.
>
> Would you have a box of cigarettes on the sideboard? And when
> the King has finished his tea you could, if you liked, ask him if he would
> smoke, as probably he would not like to smoke unless you propose it to
> him. . . As you will have to devote yourself altogether to the King, Florrie
> and I can help you by looking after the other people and I can easily see
> who wants to sit next to who.

Well ahead of the great day the roads in the Park together with the
Garden Walks were re-gravelled and the cottages fronting the Wimborne
Road at Hillbutts were all painted. Preparations were also put in hand to
ensure that all the reception rooms would be filled with flowers from the
hot houses, and the sideboards to have displays of plate.

The King had arrived at Wimborne by train from Waterloo on
Tuesday 5th December, the Wimborne Company of Volunteers, supported
by the Poole Company, forming a Guard of Honour at the Railway

Station. Having been greeted by the local dignitaries he was driven to Crichel House.

The following day was given over to a shoot when about 1,200 birds were bagged and in the morning of Thursday Viscount Portman's pack of hounds, together with many members of other hunts assembled at Crichel. Nearly every rideable horse in the district was out and those who required vehicles to follow the hunt had to pay dearly for them, so there was a very large gathering of vehicles as well as horsemen, footmen and women.

After lunch, His Majesty and a large number of the house party in five motor cars proceeded to Kingston Lacy. The route taken was through West Borough and West Street, Wimborne (both very colourful with flags and decorations), the inhabitants and school children turning out in large numbers. Hearty cheers greeted the royal party en route, and the heartiest were those which the children of Pamphill raised from their assembly point at Hillbutts, each being suitably dressed for the occasion and decorated with their County Council attendance medals

Henrietta had sent invitations to between 250 and 500 (the reports varied) friends and tenants of the Kingston Lacy and Purbeck Estates, and these assembled on the lawn to the south of the house.

The floor of the porch and steps to the front door were covered with a red carpet which had a very bright and good effect to welcome His Majesty. The King's car with His Majesty and Lady Alington arrived first, driving right up to the front door and on to the red carpet, the remaining motors pulling up just outside the porch.

The hoisting of the royal standard on the house announced the arrival of the King. He was greeted by Henrietta, her three children, Daphne, Viola, and the 'son and heir', together with Albert and Florrie Bankes. About a quarter of an hour later His Majesty appeared on the South Terrace, entered a pony carriage, and, led by Mr. Crook the head coachman, drove slowly towards the spot selected for the planting of a cedar tree, with Henrietta and little Ralph ('prettily attired in white') walking alongside. On reaching the selected spot His Majesty alighted from the carriage and smilingly handed his stick to the little squire to hold for him. The head gardener (not named in any of the reports) having placed the tree in position, the spade was then passed by Mr. Thomas Lodder, the steward of the estates, to Mr. Albert Bankes. As great uncle on behalf of the infant owner, he handed it to the King, who performed the ceremony of planting the cedar tree. The party returned to the house, tea was served and they took their departure at about 4.30 pm. His Majesty signed the visitors' book and on taking his seat in his car was loudly cheered by the guests now assembled in front of the mansion. Henrietta then invited assembled guests to 'roam over' the lawns and inspect the newly planted tree prior to tea being served in the large marquees. The guests were then welcomed inside the House (in December!), where Henrietta assisted by Albert and Florrie Bankes answered questions as to the various pictures and objet d'art. 'Time would not permit of more than a brief stay . . . in a palace of art . . . rendered brilliant by the artistic arrangements of the many electric arc lights'.

The arrangements for the visit were planned and carried out by Mr. T. Lodder (agent to the estate) assisted by Mr. A. T. Lodder and the catering for the tenancy and other guests was entrusted to Mr. C. H. Gush of Wimborne.

One can only imagine the sense of relief when the last guest had left the house, and perhaps, Henrietta, very elegantly, lowering herself down into the most comfortable armchair announcing, slightly wearily, that she would 'love a cup of tea'!

9
A Friend of the Community

FOR MOST of the following eighteen years, Henrietta would channel all her energies into the improvement and maintenance of the estate, ready for the day when at the age of twenty-one Henry John Ralph, the 'son and heir', would assume the full responsibility of his inheritance. Virtually every decision that was taken took into account the future well-being of the estate and, of course, the little squire. The focus at formal and informal events would also at some point centre on Ralph, and when the Bishop of London, having preached at Wimborne Minster, visited Kingston Lacy for lunch, before taking his leave of Henrietta and her other guests, blessed Ralph, but presumably not Daphne and Viola.

Society was still very male orientated. In his diary Albert Bankes records that also in January he went to St. James, Piccadilly to hear, again, the Bishop of London preach, but this was 'to men only'.

In certain quarters, however, women did hold their own. Albert records that he went to the Queen's Hall to hear Clara Butt sing, 'Elgar's Pomp and Circumstance song, which thrilled me'.

It was on 15th February 1906 that work started on the building of St. Stephen's Church, with the laying of the foundation stone by Henrietta, the money for the building of the Church being provided for in Walter's Will.

The event was extensively reported in the *East Dorset Herald, Dorset County Chronicle* and *Western Gazette*. The reports were all broadly similar, telling their readers that the ceremony took place:

> . . . in fine weather in the presence of a large gathering of about 500, including children from Pamphill School. Prior to the ceremony a bottle had been had been placed in a cavity in the Stone containing a copy of the *Times* [Additionally it was reported in the *Dorset County Chronicle*, a copy of that newspaper was also placed in the bottle],coins of the realm for 1906 and a document giving details of all involved in the day's events including the young squire together with Daphne and Viola.
>
> Previous to the commencement of the Service, Mrs. Bankes took up a position close to the foundation stone, her son and heir to the estates prettily attired in a white costume being by her side and holding her hand during the service and ceremony. His sisters were in close attendance also attired in white dresses. The members of the Pamphill Choir led the singing under the direction of Mrs. Shears (presiding at the harmonium).
>
> Mrs. Bankes was handed a handsome silver trowel, with which she

Foundation stone, St Stephen's (author)

assisted in the spreading of the cement and the stone having been duly lowered and proved to be properly adjusted she said 'In the faith of Jesus Christ we place this corner stone of the Church of St. Stephen in the Name of the Father and of the Son and of the Holy Ghost. Amen'.

The Archdeacon then placed his hand on the head of the little heir and said a prayer. There followed an address by the Archdeacon of Dorset and another prayer for the Church and the young heir.

The inscription on the stone reads:

THIS STONE WAS LAID BY HENRIETTE J BANKES
W[o] OF WALTER RALPH BANKES FEBRUARY 15th 1906

It is interesting to note the spelling of Henrietta's name with an E rather than an A. It would seem that, although her name is spelt with an A on her birth certificate, she preferred to use the letter E on her personal documents such as her will. Another interesting point is that no titles such as Mrs. and Mr. were used.

At the conclusion of the ceremony about 100 tenants and other guests were entertained by Henrietta at the house to tea, while a further 300 'partook of tea' in a large marquee at the school.

The trowel referred to in the report was presented to Henrietta on the previous evening. It had been subscribed for by the church workers and parishioners and is now on display in Kingston Lacy House. The inscription on the Moroccan leather case concluded:

> we are grateful for the interest you take in all that concerns your neighbours . . . an earnest prayer that God's abundant blessing may rest upon you and the young squire and his two sisters.

Although only four years old the 'young squire' was elected president of the Kingston Lacy Cricket Club at the start of the 1906 season. To celebrate his first election to a 'public' office he provided the club with bats and balls, and his mother provided caps and ties in the club colours, blue and primrose, for the players.

Throughout the summer Henrietta was in great demand to perform opening ceremonies at a number of Horticultural Society Flower Shows and other charitable events, not only in the localities where the Bankes family had traditionally always taken an interest, but also slightly further afield when she was invited to declare open the Grand Bazaar in aid of the bells of Wool Church. The Band of the 2nd Battalion, Royal Warwickshire Regiment was also in attendance!

It is too easy to underestimate the size and importance of these events in their localities. The Studland Annual Flower, Fruit, Vegetable and Industrial Show, opened by the President, Mrs. Bankes, together with the Vice President, His Grace the Duke of Hamilton in attendance, consisted of 68 classes in eight divisions with all the usual fruit, vegetables and flowers together with competitions for, 'honey baked loaf, dish of boiled potatoes, trussed fowl, duckling ready for the table, 1lb butter, dozen eggs etc'.

In the 'handicraft' classes there were opportunities for villagers to display their, 'plain and fancy needlework, assortments of coloured sand, sea shells and arrangements of seaweed. A white shirt and collar and a woollen vest,' formed part of the Laundry Work Class.

Also in the Isle of Purbeck part of Dorset, Henrietta opened the Swanage Horticultural and Industrial Flower Show (Kingston Lacy being spelt wrongly on the invitations) and the Corfe Castle Horticultural Society Show. Here entries showed a decrease on previous years, being down to 600! The show was held in the Bankes Memorial School and the Corfe Castle Band was in attendance playing selections in the school yard. Various reports inform us that:

> Mrs. Bankes was cordially thanked on the proposition by Mr. F. Cavendish-Bentinck and seconded by the Rev. Oaks. Mrs. Bankes replied in a charming little speech. . . There were three hearty cheers for Mrs. Bankes. Dancing was enjoyed in the evening.

The *Western Gazette* in its report of the Wimborne Horticultural Society Exhibition tells us that:

> Although entries and attendance did not compare favourably with previous years there was a marked improvement in the quality of exhibits staged with vegetables and honey being particularly good.
>
> Mrs. Bankes said 'I need not tell you it gives me very great pleasure to come here today to open this flower show and I am glad to think that its success is in no way dependent on anything I may say to commend it to you for I know from experience that whatever Wimborne undertakes always succeeds (hear, hear, applause). Sir John Hanham proposed a hearty vote of thanks to Mrs. Bankes . . .

There seems no doubt that Henrietta was by now very popular and very approachable. Organizers of shows and other events obviously felt confident that their invitations to her would not be ignored or dismissed and time and again her manner showed that she enjoyed helping the various organizations with their events together with being part of the occasion. She could also be generous with financial support, as demonstrated when on being elected as a Vice-President of the Isle of Purbeck and Wareham Farmers Club she made a donation of five guineas (equivalent to £320) whereas other local notables donated two or three guineas (£125 and £190).

Henrietta must have come as a 'breath of fresh air' to the estate
and the surrounding district. She was probably the first occupier of the
Kingston Lacy mansion to move amongst the local people so freely, and
to display such interest and concern in the welfare of the entire
community.

Although Henrietta was not always able to act as hostess, she did
on a number of occasions invite organizations to hold meetings in the
grounds of Kingston Lacy House. One such was the Society for the
Propagation of the Gospel, which was clearly concerned that the Society
should provide more clergy to go out to Canada:

> . . . in order to save their fellow citizens, who had gone out there from
> losing their high moral character and religious tone, as they must, if
> they were deprived of the privileges of opportunity of worship.

On another occasion, Henrietta was at the mansion to greet her
visitors. This was the annual summer outing of the Dorset Natural History
and Antiquarian Field Club during 1906. From the report of the event in
the *Dorset County Chronicle* we learn that 190 members, having visited
Wimborne Minster, then proceeded by carriages, motors, cycles and
'Chara-a-bancs' to Badbury Rings where they viewed the earthworks
followed by a picnic lunch. The party then proceeded to Kingston Lacy
where they were greeted by Henrietta supported by Albert Bankes who
as a:

> . . . gentleman of culture and travel and with the tastes and knowledge
> of the connoisseur the party had the most efficient of guides. The size
> of the party was somewhat embarrassing but Mr. Bankes performed
> his duties as cicerone with such judgement and method that the
> majority were able to see and hear clearly and well. The party were
> shown round the house then into the garden to view the exterior. Mr.
> Albert Bankes informed the gathering, when standing on the terrace,
> that the cellars were built under the entire length of it and when his
> elder brother succeeded to the property in 1856 he discovered a
> portion of the cellar bricked up and full of Port wine which had lain
> there for many years. A large percentage of the bottles had become

uncorked from age; but where the corks had remained firm the wine was quite perfect. Finally at Mrs. Bankes invitation the party then partook of tea which was served in excellent style by Mr. C. H. Gush of Wimborne.

Towards the end of September 1906, Henrietta and her three children were in the village of Corfe Castle for the ceremony of the re-opening of the reading room. This was within a property owned by Mr. Nathanial Bond and let to the managing committee for a nominal rent. The local newspaper recorded that:

> This useful Institute which is situated on a fine site facing The Square has recently been brought up to modern requirements. The large downstairs room is to be used as a recreation room. It contains some handsome pictures, a bagatelle table and a convenient table for draughts, chess and other games. Upstairs is a comfortably furnished reading room where periodicals can be found. A smaller room can be used by young people anxious to improve themselves by study.
>
> The re-opening was made a red letter day in the Parish and took place in beautiful weather. The ceremony was performed by Mrs. Bankes of Kingston Lacy who was accompanied by her two daughters and the bonny looking little Lord of the Manor. She was received at Corfe Castle by Mr. Bentinck and escorted to Morton's House. Meanwhile the Corfe Castle Town Band (under Bandmaster Stockley) had assembled outside the Bankes School where very soon the scholars from that school and the infants school were arranged in procession. Headed by the school banner they marched to The Square and formed up facing the Reading Room. Mrs. Bankes and her family were heartily received by a large crowd which had assembled in The Square where flags were freely displayed. Arriving at the door, Nora Cooper, a pupil at the Bankes School presented Mrs. Bankes with a handsome bouquet at the same time extending to her a hearty welcome to Corfe Castle.

Various speeches were then made thanking Mrs. Bankes for performing the opening ceremony and reminding everyone of the history of the reading room and its founder Rev. George Hubbard, a

Congregational Minister. During these speeches it was also stated that:

> . . . all were interested in the young heir and would follow his career with
> hope and longing that he might grow up to be a good Landlord realising
> his responsibilities.
>
> Mr. Nathanial Bond and Dr. Drury proposed and seconded a vote
> of thanks and loud cheers attested the feelings of those present. 'God
> Save the King' brought the proceedings to a loyal close.

On another occasion, this time during 1907 Kingston Lacy was host
to employed gardeners who were members of the Wimborne District
Gardeners' Association. The party of 36 reached Kingston Lacy at 4 o'clock,
presumably after a day's work, and were met by Mr. T. Lodder (Agent)
and the head gardener, (not named in any of the reports). The former
extended a welcome to the members in the absence of Mrs. Bankes, who
had not returned from Studland, where the 'little heir's birthday' was being
celebrated. After a tour of the garden, during which the members were
able to see the cedar planted by King Edward VII, and catch a glimpse of
the last of the Spanish Owls introduced about thirty years previously by
Walter Bankes, the party returned to the lawn where a 'bountiful tea was
partaken of'.

After tea the President, Mr. Luff, in expressing gratitude to Mrs.
Bankes, asked Mr. Lodder to accept on behalf of the little Squire a silver
clock and stand on the front of which was engraved: 'Presented to Henry
John Ralph Bankes by the members of the Wimborne District Gardeners'
Mutual Improvement Association on the occasion of their visit to Kingston
Lacy 15th July 1907. The head gardener was congratulated on the highly
creditable condition of the garden, although he still did not qualify to be
named in any of the reports!

In October of the following year another group of visitors arrived,
as the *Dorset County Chronicle* reported:

> Thanks to the kind invitation of Mrs. Bankes about 20 Officials engaged
> at Waterloo and Wimborne Stations spent a very enjoyable day at
> Kingston Lacy. They were met at Wimborne Station, and, favoured with
> fine weather a pleasant drive was much appreciated. Luncheon and tea

were provided for the guests who also much enjoyed the art treasures of the house.

How times have changed.

10

Another Eventful Year

THE YEAR 1907 would be no different from its predecessors, as it was to be a very busy and important year for Henrietta. In February she was invited to unveil the portrait of Canon Hart Dyke, an occasion which would mark the completion of the new Church House, in Wimborne, the foundation stone of which she had laid in 1905.

The *Dorset County Chronicle & Somersetshire Gazette* dated 14th February 1907 reported that it had been:

> . . . generally conceded that a very large portion of the success with which the Church House Scheme has been carried out has been due to the constant application to the secretarial duties, personal supervision and personal influence of Canon P Hart Dyke. From the time he was elected by the Committee as Honorary Secretary, and previously, it appears to have been his one great object to see the present excellent building erected and the liability thereby discharged.
>
> The Portrait was unveiled on Friday afternoon by Mrs. Bankes of Kingston Lacy House in the presence of the majority of the Committee and personal friends of the Canon . . . the most juvenile of which was the 'little' squire of Kingston Lacy'. During the speeches reference was made to Mrs. Bankes readily agreeing to lay the Foundation Stone on 13th September 1905 and that she had been in close touch with every detail of the work since.

The Vicar then proposed a vote of thanks to Mrs. Bankes, referring to the great interest she had shown in the town since she had arrived in the area.

St Stephen's Church, present day (author)

Although Henrietta was to receive a royal guest to Kingston Lacy at the end of the year, the event that took place on Saturday 27th July 1907 was probably the highlight of the year, if not one of the high points in her life. It was the dedication of St. Stephen's Church by the Lord Bishop of the Diocese, Bishop Wordsworth.

St. Stephen's Church was now complete. The cost of the building and fittings, together with east and north sanctuary windows, bell, organ, south transept window, frontals &c. was approximately £5,500, (equivalent to £325,000), the difference between Walter's bequest and the final cost being provided by Henrietta.

The *Dorset County Chronicle's* report dated 1st. August 1907 was some 70 column inches long, which represented approximately 17,000 words. One of the opening paragraphs stated:

> St. Stephens is 'set upon a hill' and close to these vantage grounds views can be obtained of the Minster nestling in the valley of the Stour below. The congregation of this young and vigorous offspring might therefore, as they wend their way to this beautiful modern building hear the fine

peal of bells of the ancient mother church calling her worshippers to prayer. In honour of another of her offsprings having been safely launched on its spiritual career the Union Jack was floated from the Minster's western tower and merry peals rung on Saturday when climatic conditions were all that could be desired to ensure a large attendance of those invited to participate in the opening ceremony and the after proceedings.'

Mention was made of the builder, Messrs. Hoskins & Sons of Newbury, who through their, 'able and courteous clerk of the works, Mr. W. Male', carried out the work of construction in a 'most satisfactory and commendable manner' from the plans of Mr. Ponting FSA, the Diocesan Architect. The laying out of the grounds and fencing, making up of the roads etc. was carried out by workmen on the estate under the supervision of Mr. Lodder, the agent. Full details were then given of all the gifts to the Church and of the dedication service itself which concluded with a collection which totalled £13-19s-6d. (£850).

The occasion drew to a close when:

> . . . over 200 persons were entertained to tea, at the beautiful grounds of Kingston Lacy, by Mrs. Bankes. Tables were laid out in a tent beneath several of the very fine trees and in close proximity of the house. Whilst the most tasty confections were being partaken of, the excellent band of Mr. Churcher of Bournemouth played a nice selection of music.

During the following day, Sunday, four services took place in the new church, commencing at 8.30 am with the Sacrament followed at 11.00 am with Matins Litany, 'The Bishop preached an excellent Sermon' Albert Bankes tells us. At 3.30 pm four local babies were christened by the Bishop, 'all screaming in discord' according to his diary. One presumes that did not include the Bishop!

The day drew to a close with Canon Eldon Bankes preaching 'charmingly' at the 6.30 pm service. Albert noted that he 'attended all four services and very sleepy in evening in consequence'.

Two days later on July 30th a special service took place in the church presumably for those people who were unable to be accommodated at the dedication service. This was followed by tea on the lawn at Kingston

Lacy. It would seem that no expense was spared on any of these celebrations, all being centred on the Kingston Lacy part of the estate.

However towards the end of September a letter arrived on the desk of Mr. A. T. Lodder at the Estate Office in Hillbutts. It was headed Corfe Castle and dated 24th September:

> Dear Sir, I am instructed by the Parish Council to write to you as Agent for the Trustees of the Bankes Estate to call your attention to the inadequate water supply of the village and to ask you to inform the Trustees of the urgent necessity of some steps being taken to provide the inhabitants with a better supply many of them being without any at all.

The resolution which had been passed unanimously was then quoted. The letter concluded:

> Trusting you will give the subject your immediate attention.
> Yours obediently
> E G F Smith
> Clerk to the Council

On 9th November of that year the estate trustees met the Corfe Castle Parish Council at Corfe Castle to discuss a scheme for a water supply for the town. Much correspondence followed. Then in a letter dated April 2nd 1909 from 'J. Mullins & Sons, Water Finders by the Divining Rod, Engineers & Water Works Contractors', they informed Mr. Lodder that;

> Following our Mr. Mullins visit to Corfe Castle we have to report as follows: On going to Townsend and making a thorough survey round the existing well we are of the opinion that a supply of water may be found at a depth not exceeding 25ft and will yield approximately 1,500 gallons a day but we do not think you can rely on this the whole year round but you may expect from Mr. Mullins' indications about 1,000 gallons per day in the droughty season. He also surveyed the adjacent fields but could not find anything strong enough or at a suitable depth for the requirements of the cottages or the Bankes Arms Hotel . . .

Parts of the village of Corfe Castle finally got a mains water supply in 1921, fourteen years after the initial letter was sent to the estate, although it was not until after World War II that the entire village was connected to the mains.

The year 1907 also closed with a royal visit, this time His Imperial Majesty Kaiser Wilhelm II, who was staying at Highcliffe Castle, near Christchurch.

As soon as Henrietta knew of the impending visit she sent a telegram to Albert Bankes informing him that, 'The German Emperor is coming over to tea on Sunday next. Will you and Florrie come and meet him.'

The Emperor arrived with 'a large suit' and, as with the visit of King Edward VII, planted a cedar tree in the presence of (according to the agent, Mr. Lodder) Mrs. Bankes, her family and a large number of tenants. This was followed by afternoon tea in the mansion.

In her book, *Why Not?*, Viola observed:

> My mother and the Kaiser felt an immediate attraction to each other. Her fluent German delighted him although his English was very rapid and piquantly foreign. He was very German in his frank admiration of feminine beauty and my mother was at that time extremely good looking.

It would also seem that, according to Mr. Lodder's book: 'At a later date he took tea with Mrs. Bankes at her London house, and later she was invited to a large luncheon party at the German Embassy'.

That was the last time that a ruling monarch would visit Kingston Lacy although the Princess of Wales, later to become Queen Mary, visited the house and Corfe Castle in 1908.

It was on October 14th of that year that the visit took place, the Prince and Princess of Wales staying with the Earl and Countess of Shaftesbury at Wimborne St. Giles for a week's shooting. The Princess with the ladies of the house arrived at Kingston Lacy at about 12 o'clock and were received by Mrs. Bankes, Lord and Lady Digby and Mr. and Mrs. Albert Bankes of Wolfeton House. Viola recalls the visit in *Why Not?*:

> When Queen Mary came to lunch with us at Kingston Lacy she was already thoroughly informed about the story of Corfe Castle . . . I was a little embarrassed being quite a young thing when HRH patted me on the shoulder in the kindest way and enquired 'Is she always as good as she

looks?' 'No' said my mother truthfully, 'that is the good one' indicating my sister who was known amongst ourselves as 'Miss Toogood' . . . The Princess' voice surprised me as it was rather deep for such a young woman and sounded very German. She showed real interest in us, our ages and accomplishments, and seemed so much more genuine in her questions than the usual friends of one's parents whose enquiries are purely formal.

After seeing the house and pictures, HRH planted a Liquidamber tree on the lawn near the sunken garden and, following lunch, the Princess accompanied by Mrs. Bankes and the other ladies motored to Corfe Castle where an inspection was made of the ruins and photographs of them purchased. Mr. R. Beaverstoke, the caretaker, conducted the party round. Tea was partaken of at the *Bankes Arms* – 'a quaint old inn in the village', and on leaving, the school children lined the route from the village.

It was obviously a memorable occasion for Albert Bankes as he recorded in his diary that:

> I had the great honour and pleasure of being told by Jennie to take the Princess (of Wales) into Luncheon which was laid on the big round table in the large dining room. The Princess was rather shy but made herself most agreeable.

There is no doubt that the visit of the Princess was a great success. Whether HRH or Henrietta knew of the others' birthday is something that we shall never know. It would not be surprising if they were both aware of the date that each other was born, but it was probably not commented upon.

11

The Little Squire's Inheritance

As was stated in the previous chapter the maintenance and improvement of the estate was, in Henrietta's mind, paramount. In his book covering the minority years of Henry John Ralph, hereafter referred to as Ralph, Alfred Thomas Lodder, the Agent of the Estate notes that:

> . . . the many alterations, improvements and additions carried out on the Estates during the Minority were largely due to her initiative and the great interest she always took in their management.

One must remember that the estate was at that time considerably larger than when it was bequeathed to the National Trust in 1981, and communication was limited to letters (only two deliveries a day!) and personal visits.

'Life must go on' is a phrase that is often used in difficult times and it was certainly true during the years of Walter's failing health and subsequent death. We learn from Mr. Lodder's book that in 1904, the year of Walter's death:

> A new wing, consisting of a smoking room and cloak room, with bedroom over, was added to Pamphill Manor House; [and the following year] a room for use as a Post Office, with a bedroom over was built a the end of Harmony Terrace, and two Almshouses and Reading room were also built in Studland.

Corfe Castle, thanks to the coming of the railway, was by now an important visitor attraction. The turnstiles had to be repaired and lavatories were constructed near the Martyrs' Gate within the Castle grounds. Albert Bankes' Diary also records that, 'Sergeant Baverstock, a magnificent specimen of a retired Dorset County policeman in height and size appointed Warden of Corfe Castle.' Meanwhile the whole of the electric light plant at Kingston Lacy House was overhauled.

Back in the 1880s a correspondent referring, in one of the local newspapers, to 'Sandbanks Inn' observed:

> How on earth it should have occurred to any human being to build an Inn on the end of the dreary spit of sand that marks the entrance to Poole Harbour must remain a mystery.
>
> It is miles distant from anywhere and with the exceptions of

yachtsmen in summer and perhaps some wild fowl shooters in winter its guests can scarcely be numerous.

But the pressures of modern day 'progress' were making themselves felt on the estate when, in 1906, Mr. Lodder records, 'An enquiry was held at Bournemouth as to the powers sought by a Company called "The Swanage Light Railway Co.", to construct a Conveyor Bridge at South Haven and a Light railway across Studland Heath'.

Thankfully neither was built. The maintenance and building on the estate continued unabated throughout 1906:

> Rain water tanks and water supply pipes were provided to various farms. Cart horse stables, hack stables and coach house built at Cowgrove Farm. Exterior and interior of greenhouses at the Gardens painted by contractors and additional greenhouses erected by Mrs. Bankes on North wall of the Gardens.
>
> A number of cowsheds, piggeries, cowstalls and cart sheds built on various farms at Kingston Lacy and Studland.
>
> Erected five houses called Church Terrace, Corfe Castle.

Probably the biggest single undertaking beyond Kingston Lacy was the complete overhaul of the entire Manor House at Studland which today we would refer to as their holiday home. Gas was laid on and central heating installed. Buildings in the grounds were converted to coachman's, groom's, gardener's and chauffeur's cottages and by June 1908 Albert and Florrie Bankes were shown, 'over the Manor House which is quite ready for the furniture the painters having finished it. I am very pleased with all the exterior and the interior is spick and span clean from top to bottom'.

Plans for most of the building work on the estate, including of course Pamphill Church, were drawn up by Mr. C. E. Ponting. Preparations for the refurbishment of the Manor House were no exception, and the building work in this case was undertaken by George Hardy of Swanage. The *Manor House Hotel*, as it is today, is well worth a visit for either a holiday or just a meal.

At the other end of the social scale Henrietta arranged for a new pavilion to be built for Pamphill Cricket Club and horse boxes at

Abbottstreet were converted into a miniature rifle range, a reading room being added to the end of the range some while later!

Having built new cow stalls and storage facilities at Priory Farm (part of Crab Farm) for Mr. P. C. Tory the old cow stalls next to the church at Shapwick were then converted into a rifle range.

The *Dorset County Chronicle* during February 1909 reported that:

> On Monday Mrs. Bankes opened a Rifle range which she has kindly provided for the use of the young men of Shapwick. . . The range is 25 yards long, of excellent width with boarded sides and corrugated iron roof. Cow pens formally occupied the site. . . The cost of the range has been provided by Mrs. Bankes who to celebrate the opening invited all adults of the Parish to tea after she had performed the opening function . . . As a result of the first shot fired by Mrs. Bankes an inner was registered by the markers. Mrs. Bankes gave a short speech and Mr. Kent on behalf of the large gathering thanked Mrs. Bankes and the Trustees. Hearty cheers were given for Mrs. Bankes and also for 'the little squire' . . . After the opening the company adjourned to the schoolroom where about 190 adults partook of the excellent tea provided by Mr. J. D. Bradley of Wimborne. It is the first parochial function held in the schools since they have been rebuilt . . . few villages can boast better scholastic buildings. Mrs. Bankes, Mrs. and the Misses Cave, Mr. Tory, Mr. Lodder, Mrs. House. Miss Drake, Miss Kent and other ladies kindly assisted at the urns . . . The room was cleared and at six o'clock an amusing cinematograph entertainment was given, after some excellent pictures of the little Squire, Mrs. Bankes, and her children had been shown on the screen.

The 'little Squire' was invariably in attendance with his mother on these occasions and one gets the impression that Henrietta was anxious that he should learn his responsibilities to his tenants and the local community as part of his inheritance.

Although the ranges are no longer there, the cricket pavilion served the club well over the years and was recently refurbished and extended by the estate with many of the original features being carefully included in the final design.

Fire damage to property was a constant concern in the rural areas with oil lamps for lighting and coal together with wood being the main fuel for heating and cooking. The estate seemed to have had its fair share of problems, with reports of houses, cottages and other buildings being engulfed by flames. This usually resulted in total loss of the building, not to mention the loss of the tenants' personal belongings and possibly of their livelihood.

Buildings and the farmhouse at Leigh Farm were all damaged by fire in 1907 and the dairy house at Manor Farm, Studland was destroyed in 1908. Framptons Cottages at Mannington and Middleton's House in Colehill all had to be rebuilt. Lightning struck the newly built stables at Cowgrove Farm; and Bothenwood Farm in Holt, together with Snag House Farm on Norden Heath, were both destroyed by fire.

In 1909 it was the turn of Kingston Lacy House to undergo a major refurbishment with extensive alterations and additions to the sanitary systems and drainage. Again we turn to Mr. A. T. Lodder's book covering the 'Minority Years' to learn that during this work four extra baths, six WCs, together with the inevitable additional septic tanks, were installed. The central heating system was extended and a new boiler was installed – these were just some of the works undertaken.

But, round about this time the focus of attention was suddenly switched to the little 'squire himself, when the local newspapers reported the:

> ILLNESS OF THE 'SQUIRE: The utmost anxiety was occasioned throughout the district when it became known that Master Henry Ralph Bankes, the little 'squire of Kingston Lacy was dangerously ill and that an operation for appendicitis was necessary. The sincere sympathy of the inhabitants went out to his mother, Mrs. Bankes in her severe trial and the tradesmen's windows at Wimborne where bulletins were displayed were frequently visited.

The operation was performed at Dr. Scott's Nursing Home in Bournemouth and happily proved successful. It was obviously a great relief to the whole neighbourhood to learn that the little patient was improving and had sufficiently recovered as to render further bulletins unnecessary.

Henrietta and the Little Squire (National Trust)

Appendicitis is today still serious and life-threatening, but in the early part of the 20th century the additional concern was whether the patient, and particularly one so young, would survive the effects of the anaesthetic, which to everyone's great relief he did.

Life on the estate then settled back into its busy routine. As we saw with the comments earlier concerning the school at Shapwick, the education facilities in the area were not forgotten, and now the Pamphill School building was improved and a new infant's classroom built. The estate trustees also provided money for the enlargement of schools in Purbeck. During 1911 Henrietta purchased a pair of cottages opposite the church at Shapwick, and these were then converted into a reading room together with accommodation for a caretaker.

It was probably in the latter part of the Edwardian period that Henrietta created a Japanese Garden within the grounds of Kingston Lacy House. This form of gardening had become very fashionable and many gardens throughout the country followed the trend. By the time the National Trust inherited the Estate in 1983 there was little or no evidence, on the ground, of the garden ever having existed, neither was there much archive material to guide anyone planning a restoration. A geophysical survey was undertaken on what was believed to be the site of the Tea Garden but the results were inconclusive. However, undeterred, the present Head Gardener, Nigel Chalk, with funding from the Gordon Bulmer Charitable Trust, together with a small group of hard working gardeners, set about recreating a garden in the Japanese tradition. The new garden we see today is full of symbolic representations, together with what might have been a British Edwardian interpretation of a Japanese garden. It is well worth a visit, particularly to see it in its early stages of maturity.

Henrietta was single-minded in her belief that the Bankes family should own and live on the estate for ever, and when Ralph became twenty-one and formally inherited the property she would hand over to him an inheritance that would be materially and socially in as good a condition as it was possible for it to be.

Viola, in her book *Why Not?*, recalls that on one occasion during this period Mr. Selfrdge, the owner of the department store, and friend of the family, enquired of their mother, 'Why not put the boy into business?' adding that he would, 'give him a start in the Selfridge Stores!' 'Why should he?' my mother would reply, with maddening calm. 'The Bankes' have lived in this fashion for generations, and I hope my boy will carry on the tradition.'

Whether Henrietta ever really 'handed over the reins' to her son is, as we shall see later, a matter for conjecture. But she certainly exercised great influence right up until the time that Ralph married in 1935, and possibly to a lesser extent after that.

12

Difficult Times, Changing Times

WYNNE ALBERT BANKES, Henrietta's 'Uncle in Law' and one of the trustees of the estate during Ralph's minority, died in April 1913 one month short of his seventy-third birthday.

It must have been a very sad moment for Henrietta when she received the news of his death, as it would seem that he was one of the few people she could trust and rely on. She must have felt very lonely at that moment. Albert, and his wife Florrie, had been a great support to Henrietta, always ready to give help and advice when asked for but never, it would seem, to intrude into her personal life.

Albert was very conscious of his social responsibilities and put a great deal of effort and time into supporting Charminster Parish Church, as well as helping the less fortunate members of the local community. He was also one of the driving forces behind the creation and establishment of the Dorset County Museum in Dorchester, and the building at Herrison's Fields of the Hospital which now, being no longer needed for its original purpose, is being converted into a new complete village community. He was also a member of Weymouth Yacht Club, and was persistent in his efforts during the late 1870s to get the club rules changed to allow ladies to be admitted for lunch and tea. This was finally agreed to in August 1880.

Wynne Albert was buried along with many other members of the Bankes family in Studland churchyard.

The First World War, the 'Great War', commenced on August 4th 1914. In relation to the numbers of people living in the areas, it probably had a far greater impact on rural communities than on towns and cities, because of the larger proportion of men volunteering and eventually being called up, together with those who were killed.

Alfred Thomas Lodder, who was the resident agent on the estate, left to rejoin his regiment on August 11th and was absent until 2nd February 1918. His father Thomas Lodder, the previous agent, took over his duties but unfortunately died during May 1916. Due to the shortage of men on the estate only essential tasks were carried out. One of these was the rebuilding of Bothenwood Farmhouse at Holt, together with a water supply and a wind engine to pump the water to the farmyard and house. The farm is not now part of the estate but one can still see the plaque, although somewhat eroded, on the farmhouse wall, inscribed 'HRB 1918'.

The 'Great War' ended on 11th November 1918 and the estate, as with the entire nation, had to come to terms with the enormous loss of life on the battlefields. Seven men from the parish of Shapwick, eleven men from Studland and sixteen from Pamphill, including a father and his two sons, were killed during the hostilities. The following year, 1919, land from various farms on the estate was let to Dorset County Council for the re-settlement of ex-servicemen, and there was, according to Mr. Lodder; 'much industrial unrest and many strikes'.

Also at this time a large quantity of pit props was cut and sold by the estate, and despatched to the Welsh collieries. Plans for building workmen's dwellings at Pamphill, Shapwick, Colehill and Corfe Castle were prepared, although only in the case of Corfe Castle were cottages built.

But by far the single biggest event took place in the autumn when it was announced that:

> BY ORDER OF THE TRUSTEES OF KINGSTON LACY AND CORFE CASTLE A Valuable Freehold Agricultural Estate in the Parish of Holt East, to be sold by Auction at the Victoria Hall Wimborne Dorset September 10 and 11 1919. The value of the Estate for building purposes is greatly enhanced by the beauty of the surrounding scenery. Comprising of upwards of 1,800 Acres including Ten Farms varying from 50–300 Acres. 55 Small Holdings and Parcels of Arable and Pasture Land varying in extent from 5-30 Acres. About 70 Cottages all with good gardens and the majority with Arable or Pasture Plots attached varying from half an acre to three acres. . . There are 6 Woods to be offered in separate lots containing a total area of 170 Acres of excellent Oak Timber easily accessible by good roads.

What prompted the Trustees, which included Henrietta, to offer the property and land for sale is not clear, but the auction was obviously a major event lasting two days with substantial farms such as, Pig Oak, Holt Lodge, Bothenwood (where only the previous year had the farmhouse been rebuilt), Holt Green and Vicarage all going 'under the hammer'. The total amount realised from the sale was £57,071 (1919 values) which represents about £1.5 million in today's values, but not current property values.

The First World War was still casting its shadow over the country, as it would for many years to come. It was in 1920 that land in Colehill was given to the parish by the estate for the site of a war memorial, and the following year, 1921, Ralph performed what was probably his first formal public duty when he unveiled a memorial in St. Stephen's Church, Pamphill to the local men who had died in 'The Great War' or 'The War to End All Wars', as it was so often referred to.

It was also in that year the village of Corfe Castle was finally connected to a mains water supply, fourteen years after the initial letter was sent to the estate.

The following year, 1922, the Rev. D'Ewes Benison was instituted as the first vicar of St. Stephen's, Kingston Lacy, after the ecclesiastical parish had been established and Henrietta had provided an endowment of £6,000 secured to the benefice of St. Stephen's. The Ecclesiastical Commissioners gave £400 for the enlargement of the vicarage house.

In the same year negotiations took place between the estate and the Bournemouth and Swanage Motor Road & Ferry Company for the building of a road from Studland to South Haven and the establishment of a ferry from North Haven to South Haven. These discussions were inconclusive and the company sought powers through an Act of Parliament, which were obtained in 1923 and changed the face of Studland for ever. No doubt, Henrietta followed the discussions with great interest, concerned as always with the effect they would have on the estate which Ralph would inherit in the same year.

13
Celebrations

T HE YEAR 1923, and what a memorable year it was to be for the nation, and for Henrietta!

It was in the April of that year that Prince Albert, the Duke of York, married Lady Elizabeth Bowes-Lyon, spending part of their honeymoon at what is now another National Trust property, Polesden

Lacey. They would not have had the slightest idea that with the abdication of his brother, Edward VIII in December 1936, Prince Albert would become King and be known as George VI, with his wife becoming Queen Elizabeth, to become known in more recent times as the Queen Mother. Also in 1923, the English FA Cup Final was played at Wembley for the first time, with the now famous photograph of one policeman on his white horse controlling the crowd which had encroached on to the pitch.

But more importantly for Henrietta we have arrived at the year and the event which she would probably see as the climax of everything that she had been working for since the death of her husband Walter Ralph Bankes in 1904, her beloved son attaining his majority and all that went with it.

The garden party to celebrate Ralph's coming of age took place on Wednesday August 1st. There must have been quite a few weeks of frenetic preparation for the occasion, with the booking of the band of the Royal Marine Artillery from Portsmouth at a cost of twenty-five guineas for twenty players, plus rail expenses, and of thirteen coaches from Shamrock Motor Coaches to bring 317 guests from Purbeck. Then there was arranging for the supply of the marquees from Piplers of Poole, and the catering arrangements to be provided by Gush's Restaurant of Wimborne. Mr. Ricketts of the *Vine* public house in Pamphill was to supply the beer and minerals (£29 9s. od.) and Marstons, Dolphin Brewery Co., the whiskey (£13 15s. od.) for consumption in the refreshment tents. The services of the police and special constables were arranged (£6 2s. od.) but the AA stated that they were not able to assist in the parking of cars at the garden party, as they would be unable to withdraw any of their men from patrols.

The writing and posting of approximately 1,600 invitations and, of course, the processing of the replies must have been a very time-consuming operation. Additionally each person accepting the invitation was then sent an admission card.

The party was fully reported in the (Bournemouth) *Daily Echo*, and from it we learn that the day of the party had dawned bright and sunny and remained so all day. While the guests were partaking of tea

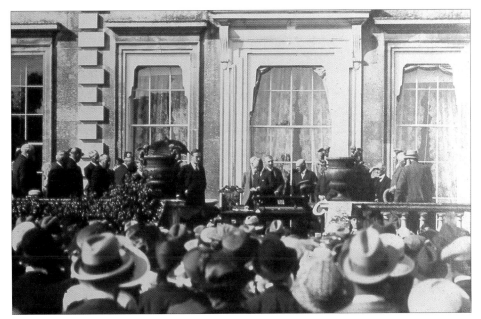

Ralph's coming of age party, 1923: the Presentations (National Trust)

the Royal Marines Band played a selection of music including excerpts from *Merrie England* and *The Beggars Opera*!

After tea was over the company adjourned to the terrace, and here the various presentations were made. The first, from the town of Wimborne and the neighbourhood, was presented by Mr. R. Cribb, Chairman of the Wimborne Urban District Council.

The gifts were a very handsome solid silver inkstand, a silver blotter, two silver candlesticks and a silver seal. These were accompanied by an album in blue and gold colours, containing an address on vellum with the names of about 400 subscribers attached.

Mr. Cribb, after reading the address, apologised for taking the liberty of adding a few words, it being:

> . . . a day long to be remembered. He referred to the great care and anxiety spent upon Mr. Bankes by his noble and worthy mother from the cradle right up to the present time, and said he felt sure that that great and anxious care which had been so given would not be wasted. (Applause) In conclusion he hoped that he (Mr. Bankes) would give them

the opportunity presently of tasting his wedding cake. The last remark was received with a great outburst of cheering.

The gift of the tenant farmers on estates was a fine breech-loading gun, and Mr. D. W. Kent in making the presentation on behalf of the tenant farmers said it, 'would afford good sport and in conclusion he hoped Mr. Bankes would one day marry a nice wife and would reside among them for many years to come. (Cheers)'.

The Rev. E. Benison, vicar of Kingston Lacy, on behalf of all the tenants, except Studland, made the presentation to the squire of a gold cigarette case and an address which was contained in a red morocco album. Its outer covers were ornamented in gold with the monogram H.J.R.B., and the album also contained the names of about 500 of his tenants.

Mr. Stanley, an old tenant, presented to Mr. Bankes on behalf of the Studland tenants a 'gold chair', adding in broad Dorset: 'I hope ee ull be pleased wi un'. (Laughter and applause) The chair it would seem was a real work of art, manufactured in Dorset with the leather and woodwork all originating from Dorset.

Next came Mr. Alfred Lodder, the agent, who said that on behalf of the estate staff, 'they felt great honour to serve under him . . . . a long and happy life that ere long they would see him married and that later when they saw him in the park in his motor they would see a perambulator going up and down as well.' (Cheers).

The 46 employees of the estate had subscribed £11 2s. 6d. with contributions ranging from £2 5s. 6d. from Mr. Lodder down to 1s. 6d., although most were 2s. 6d. with some at 10s. With the money collected J. E. Beale of Bournemouth (30 departments, Tel. Bournemouth 1) was commissioned to provided an, 'Illuminated Testimonial to include a sketch in water colour on Whatman Board in a polished oil frame'.

The presentation ceremony came to an end when:

Mr. Bankes, who addressed his audience as my dear friends, said his first duty was to express thanks to one and all for coming. . . He took the opportunity also of thanking his trustees, Mr. George Harvey and Sir John Bankes. Sir John was unable to be present, but he was glad to see his son among them. . . Last, but not least he thanked them very much for the reference to his dear mother. No words of his could ever express his thanks for her solicitude for and loving care and kindness to him during the time of his minority. (Applause) . . . and in reference to hopes expressed with regard to his taking a wife he said he should not disappoint them. (Cheers). Cheers were given again for Mr. Bankes and for Mrs. and the Misses Bankes. Mrs. Bankes in responding said she was glad to see all who were present that day and she hoped they would spend a pleasant evening. The party broke up shortly after seven o'clock after the spending of a most pleasant and enjoyable time.

Although there was to be another garden party in 1937, nothing on the scale of this celebration of Ralph's coming of age would ever happen again.

14
Squire Bankes

Having reached the age of twenty-one, or as it is sometimes known, his majority, Henry John Ralph Bankes was the owner in all senses of the word of the Kingston Lacy and Corfe Castle Estate. But to what extent Henrietta 'handed over the reins' to her son is debatable, as we shall see later from correspondence concerning the Estate.

During the autumn of 1926 Ralph drove his motor-bike, with his sister Viola riding pillion, to call on the writer Thomas Hardy at his home, 'Max Gate' near Dorchester, and they invited him, and his wife Florence to tea at Kingston Lacy. The invitation was accepted and the visit duly took place in September. It would seem from the Kingston Lacy archives that the visit was a great success, a photograph of a smiling Thomas Hardy taken during the afternoon later being displayed on one of the writing desks in Kingston Lacy House.

A few days later Florence Hardy sent a 'thank you' letter, dated 30th September and addressed to Daphne:

> We both so much enjoyed that delightful time we had with you. TH loved his visit. If at any time you would like his opinion on any MS of yours I should be most pleased to read it aloud to him and tell you exactly what he thinks of it. His judgement is still very sound.

It would appear that Henrietta was not present on this occasion and it is possible that, in common with some sections of society at the time, she did not approve of Thomas Hardy's writings, particularly after the publication of *Jude the Obscure*.

The following month, October 1926, the parishioners living in and around Pamphill were determined not to miss the opportunity to enjoy themselves, and, according to the *Kingston Lacy Parish Magazine*, to celebrate the:

> Opening of the Parish Hall – Whist Drive and Dance. Whist drive commenced 7.00pm with 128 sitting down, many others came in later for dancing which commenced at 11 o'clock and lasted to nearly 2.00am.

Present day regulations would not allow an event of this size to take place in the hall, it being limited to accommodate only eighty people.

According to Viola in the book *A Kingston Lacy Childhood* it was in the spring of the following year that an irreconcilable rift took place between Viola and her mother Henrietta. It would seem a very real concern, one of which all mothers of young daughters in this stratum of society would be familiar, that her daughter would marry into a titled family and enjoy an enhanced status in society, as well as a very comfortable and secure lifestyle. However Viola had decided to marry an untitled Australian doctor, apparently to the total disapproval of her mother. We shall never know what Henrietta's true feelings were on this occasion. She may have been the more disappointed because she knew how many of the neighbouring modestly titled and in some cases untitled families had seen their daughters marry into some of the nation's very wealthy and powerful families. They included 'Uncle' Albert Bankes' daughter, Gladys, who married into the Stucley family. Her husband, Sir Hugh Stucley succeeded to the title 4th Bart., and Henrietta's own sister, Jessie, in marrying Sir Bourchier Wrey had become Lady Wrey.

As was stated earlier, it is difficult to judge to what extent Henrietta still 'held the reins', but as we see from the following correspondence, from Mr. A T Lodder, the agent, all addressed to 'Mrs. Bankes' at her London home, it is not unreasonable to assume that she was the prime decision-maker on most if not all matters concerning the running of the estate.

The first extract is taken from a letter dated 30th November 1933:

> . . . Mr. and Mrs. Parry-Evans at Vicarage. . . Kitchen range and bath replacement. . . New porcelain bath £5.0.0 and small kitchen range £12 . . . Suggest leave the whole matter until you are next at Kingston Lacy . . . Kerridge has repaired the Hall Clock. . . New bungalow at Corfe Castle has the new tiles on. . . I think you will be pleased with it. . .

The second extract comes from a letter dated 4th December 1933 and Mr. Lodder enquires:

> . . . if I am to continue Christmas gifts. . . last year were:
>
> Pamphill Slate Club   £2.0.0
> Employees   2/6 each
> St. Margarets Almspeople   5/- each
> Gillinghams   2/6 each
> Coal to Studland poor   3 cwt each
> Coal to Shapwick poor   4 cwt each
> Kingston Lacy Rifle
> Club's Christmas Shoot   £1.0.0
> Tea etc to Studland School Children'

Another letter, also dated 4th December 1933, reads: 'I have no doubt Mr. Bankes mentioned to you that Mr. Bentley Carr wished to surrender the lease of Pamphill Manor House . . .'.

In a further letter dated 11th December 1933, Mr. Lodder informs Henrietta: 'I am in receipt of your letter this morning regards the grate and bath at the Vicarage. . . I will make use of the old bath and grate and will give you credit for their value'.

At this point in the letter one feels that Mr. Lodder bristles with indignation, barely containing his annoyance:

> I also saw in the *Western Gazette* the reference to the new farm house which is being erected for Mr. Crofts (not Marsh) at Vineyard Farm, Corfe Castle. The notification in the paper was the first intimation I had that there was anyone objecting to the house as I have several people comment upon the suitability of the house for the site. I do not know the man from Bournemouth who wrote the letter to the Council, but feel it is his own personal views and I must say I rather resent his interference. Most of these Societies are made up of half pay Officers and retired tradesmen who go around the country airing their views on matters of which they have very little knowledge, at the expense of the landowners, and think the landowners should hold up the whole of their land for them to roam over at their pleasure, for which they pay nothing. Any reasonable person would realise to farm a 100 acre farm it is necessary there should be a farm house and I am sure you and all of us, had the welfare of the district in our minds when selecting the plan and finish for this particular house and surroundings, and when complete with dark tiles and grey rough casting it cannot be offensive to the eye.

Mr. Lodder continues, his composure restored:

> Stewarts sent the cedar tree . . . awaiting your return to Kingston Lacy. . . let me know the exact position you wish it to be planted. I was at Kingston Lacy this morning and warned them in the house to be careful not to allow the taps or bath to drip. . .

Finally on 13th December 1933, Mr. Lodder writes: '. . . colour of rough cast on farm house at Corfe Castle. . . I propose having a small panel done with the grey rough casting for you and Mr. Bankes to see, and you can then decide. . . '

Ten years after he attained his majority it would seem that 'Squire Bankes' was still taking second place to his mother, but a young lady from Yorkshire was about to change all that.

15
Miss Hilary Strickland-Constable

Hilary was born on the 29th October 1908 at Old Hall, Hornsea, East Yorkshire a sister for Henry Marmaduke and Robert Frederick. Their mother was Margaret Elizabeth née Pakenham, and their father was Captain, later Lt. Colonel, Frederick Charles Strickland-Constable. Soon after Hilary was born the family moved to Wassand Hall situated at Seaton, just a few miles inland from Hornsea and approximately 18 Miles north of Hull, East Yorkshire.

From the genealogy website of Nigel Batty-Smith we learn that Margaret Elizabeth, was the only child of Rear Admiral the Hon. Thomas Alexander Pakenham, son of the 2nd Earl of Longford, and Sophia Frances née Sykes, and that she, Margaret Elizabeth, married Frederick Charles Strickland-Constable during August 1898.

From archive material kindly supplied by The Prince of Wales' Own Regiment of Yorkshire, Regimental Headquarters in York we learn that Frederick Charles Strickland-Constable served as a Captain with the 3rd Battalion East Yorkshire Regiment in the Boer War from April 1902 until September 1903 and was eventually promoted to Lt. Colonel in March 1913, when he assumed command of his Battalion. The Battalion did not go over to France during World War I but remained in England providing training and reinforcements. Lt. Colonel Strickland-Constable died of pneumonia during December 1917, aged 57, whilst still serving with his Battalion.

Wassand Hall, East Yorkshire (Photograph supplied by Mr Rupert Russell)

Hilary's elder brother, Henry Marmaduke was a contemporary of Ralph Bankes at Eton and Magdalen College, Oxford and it was while Ralph was on a visit to Wassand Hall that Hilary and he became engaged.

Announcements of the engagement appeared in the *Morning Post, Times, Evening Standard, Daily Mirror, Yorkshire Post, Yorkshire Evening Post, Bournemouth Echo, Bournemouth Times & Directory, Bath Herald, Western Gazette, Poole & East Dorset Herald* and *Dorset County Chronicle,* with the *Daily Mirror, Morning Post* and *Western Gazette* reproducing portraits of Hilary.

The announcements were all broadly similar, giving details of the history of the Bankes family with an additional comment in the '*Echo*' that Ralph was a '. . . keen sportsman, President of Ferndown Golf Club and Wimborne Cricket Club'.

Unlike the announcements of Henrietta's engagement, the reports gave details of Hilary's family history with, additionally, the *Yorkshire Post* 'Social Diary' telling us that:

> . . . Miss Strickland-Constable does not claim the musical tastes of her
> brother, who studied composition at Eton – where he actually wrote

music – under the late Sir Charles Stanford and who first appeared as a composer with the Oxford Musical Union.

On the estate I have no doubt that everyone was delighted with the news that at last the 33-year-old squire was getting married. Prior to the wedding Hilary travelled down to Kingston Lacy, and there was a party in the Pamphill Village Hall at which Ralph introduced his fiancée to the villagers.

The wedding took place on 19th September 1935 in St. Lawrence's Church, Sigglesthorne, Yorkshire and was briefly reported in the *Times* and the *Bournemouth Times and Directory*. More detailed reports appeared in the *Yorkshire Post* and the *Yorkshire Evening Press*, a summary of which tells us that it was:

St Lawrence, Sigglethorne (Colin Hinson)

. . . a quiet ceremony attended only by the nearest relatives and neighbours.

The bride, who was given away by her brother Mr. Henry Marmaduke Strickland-Constable, wore a graceful oyster satin gown featuring a cowl collar effect and cut on flowing lines the skirt terminating in a long train. Her veil of Brussels lace was one which had been previously worn by her mother and grandmother and was held by a bandeau of diamonds – the gift of her mother. She carried a bouquet of shell pink carnations. There were no bridesmaids.

The honeymoon is to be spent motoring. The bride travelled in brown tweed over which she wore a brown ermine coat'.

Additionally the *Bournemouth Times and Directory* gave details of the wedding gifts which:

. . . have included four silver octagonal sweet dishes and a silver sugar caster from the tenant farmers on his home, Isle of Purbeck and Shaftesbury Estates, a leather suitcase from the estate staff of the home and Isle of Purbeck, and a silver Georgian sugar dredger from his house staff. On his return to Kingston Lacy a presentation is to be made to Mr. Bankes by his tenants in the Studland, Corfe Castle and Wimborne districts.

No mention of Mrs. Bankes!

Life and attitudes were so different then. The entire congregation had to be in the church for morning worship before the arrival of the Squire and Mrs. Bankes, and as they entered the church all would stand up. Only after Mr. and Mrs. Bankes were seated would the rest of the congregation also sit down.

Another glimpse into everyday lives at that time is told in the following extract taken from the *Bournemouth Times and Directory* dated Friday September 20th 1935 under the heading 'Wimborne':

W.I. MEETING.- Miss K. Style, J.P., presided at the monthly meeting of the Women's Institute on Thursday last week. An interesting and helpful demonstration on suit pressing was given by Mr. Edwards, of Blandford, which was much appreciated, and an exhibition of blackberry preserves was enjoyed. A charade, acted by the Misses Housden, created much amusement, and finally, the members partook of tea, served by the committee.

It is too easy, seventy and more years later, to imagine that it was a world of peace and tranquillity, but at this time in Germany decisions were being taken that would change the world. These were being reported even in the local press, but perhaps were not being taken seriously by the general population of Great Britain.

An article in the *Bournemouth Daily Echo* of September 16th 1935 was headed, 'Hitler's New Deal for Jews in Germany'. The rather frightening article concluded:

> For us the swastika has become a holy symbol for our race, as opposed to the Jews. This symbol now flies over Germany. Naturally, the Jews will not be allowed to hoist this holy flag. The whole world shall know that Germany will live for ever under this flag. Whoever insults this flag insults the nation.
>
> Referring to anti-Jewish laws, General Goering said: 'It is our duty to protect the purity of our blood against the lust of the Jewish race'. The sitting concluded with frantic cheering and the singing of the Horst Wessel song.

However on the Kingston Lacy estate Hilary was about to undertake the difficult task of taking over the running of the house from Henrietta, who had dominated the local scene for at least the previous thirty years, if not more.

It is difficult to judge what the relationship between Henrietta and Hilary was, but one would suspect that it was respectful and very polite with 'Mother in Law' not being backward in suggesting how the house should be run and Hilary patiently listening and then organizing everything in her own way.

In an extract from a letter stored in the Bankes archive and published by the National Trust on their website we learn that, on their return from their honeymoon, they (Hilary and Ralph) found a short handover letter, which concluded:

Please little Hilary, don't think me an old fuss pot, but when you have visitors staying, try to get them to rub their shoes well and not wear any with studs or nails in them as it is so injurious to the marble (floors), and gravel makes such a mess – it takes two housemaids a week or more to do the marble stairs – this is such a delicate marble . . . yours ever Henrietta.

One's first reaction to the form of address, 'little Hilary', is to see it as a 'put down' by Henrietta, but that the letter has survived perhaps indicates that possibly it was a family term of endearment that Hilary did not take exception to.

But whatever the relationship between Henrietta and Hilary was, a new era in the life of the 'Bankes Estate' was about to begin.

16

Mrs. Hilary Bankes, Lady of the House

HILARY UNDOUBTEDLY quickly set about running the house and busying herself around the estate. This included driving her car around the area during the general election of 1935, taking some of the older tenants to the polling station. As we shall see later this concern for the local inhabitants was very much part of Hilary's make-up.

However 1937 was to be a very important year for Hilary and Ralph, although the *Bournemouth Daily Echo* dated January 1st announced, 'A DEPRESSING BEGINNING TO THE NEW YEAR'. This was due to the torrential rain that 'dampened the enthusiasm' of many revellers.

However it was not all bad news on that day: 'At the close of play in the Third Test Match at Melbourne today Australia had scored 181 for 6 wickets. Bradman again disappointing and was out for 13'. At the end of January the same newspaper reported: 'Motorists snowed up on Dorset hilltop. Whole Country swept by blizzard'.

In February the, 'Ringwood and Fordingbridge District Council heard a report on the progress of the slum clearance scheme. 99 houses had been reported as being unfit for human habitation'. We should realize that this was a problem that was not just confined to that area but was spread throughout Hampshire, Dorset and beyond.

But the really important news was in the *Bournemouth Times and Directory* dated February 12th 1937 when it announced under the heading Wimborne:

> Heir for Dorset Landowner
>
> A son was born on Wednesday in a London Nursing Home to the wife of Mr. Henry John Ralph Bankes JP of Kingston Lacy and the bells of Wimborne Minster, Corfe Castle, Studland and Shapwick Churches were rung last night.

At the beginning of July preparations were being made for a garden party to be held on 25th August, presumably to celebrate the birth of baby John. 'Presumably', because nowhere on the invitation card or in any reports was there mention of the reason for the party.

The form and style of the invitation cards followed almost identically those for the 1923 and 1897 garden parties except that in the bottom left hand corner of the 1937 card we see the following: 'No children can be admitted'.

Additionally in the instructions to attendants on the coaches bringing tenants to the party from the Isle of Purbeck we read: 'No children must accompany the party under any conditions whatsoever'. Perhaps there was a disease which was infecting children, and the estate was anxious that it should not spread.

Instructions were issued and quotations for the supply of various items were sought by Major Lodder, the agent to the estate. One such quotation requested was from Piplers of Poole, the response dated July 12th 1937 being:

> Dear Sir
>
> To Hire, inclusive of delivery, erection and removal of 2 Marquees each 165' x 36' £25-0-0

Tabling for above (96 12' trestle tables) £5-0-0

Major Lodder was quickly on the telephone querying the quotation which prompted a further letter from Piplers:

Dear Sir
Following your call of this morning re our quotation for the Hire of Marquees.

As regards the price quoted in 1923 compared with our present quotation we would point out that values both of labour and materials have risen so considerably since then that we are unable to supply at the same figure as in 1923.

In order to meet you in the matter, however we are willing to make the charge for the hire of the two marquees £22-10-0 instead of our original figure of £25-0-0 but this is the very best we can do.'

Mr. E H Ricketts of the *Vine Inn* Pamphill received his orders from Major Lodder:

Dear Sir
With reference to my interview with you regarding the garden party to be held at Kingston Lacy on 25th August; I write to confirm that I shall be glad if you will provide the beer and minerals as you did on a previous occasion. I shall require the following:-
2 – 36 gallon casks of bitter beer
1 – 18 gallon cask of bitter beer
15 cases of mixed minerals

The beer I require you to supply is that retailed to the public at 7d per pint, and I shall be glad if you will make it quite clear to Messrs. Strong & Co. that this is the quality I require.

In another note arrangements were made for a horse and cart to be available to transport the casks.

The music for the occasion was provided by the Bournemouth Military Band:

I can supply a first Class Band of 20 Professional Musicians in uniform and Conductor.

Hilary, Ralph and Baby John
(photograph supplied by Mrs Sybil Rhodes)

Terms: Twenty Two Guineas £23.2.

Plus Travelling and Transport expenses'

There were twenty items of music on the programme which included the march *Old Comrades* followed by various selections from *The Mikado* and *Sweethearts of Yesterday* and these were followed by more marches including *Colonel Bogey*. The programme concluded with *Bells Across the Meadow* and the *Dorsetshire Regimental March*. The printed programme for display was on cards identical to the one used for the 1923 party.

The Party was reported the following day on an inside page of the *Bournemouth Daily Echo*, announcing that there was a: 'Garden Party at Kingston Lacy, Mr. and Mrs. Ralph Bankes' 1,000 guests'. The brief report itself ran to only 182 words.

On another inside page an article commented that: 'Television makes headway. . . Southern people awaiting it. . . How and when will the BBC satisfy that demand. . . When the BBC cares to give it.'

But on the front page of the same newspaper its readers learnt that:

A 28-year-old German girl, 'blonde, good housewife and a keen sportswomen,' has written to Corporal W. Crawley of the military hospital at Netley, Southampton, following his letter to the Mayor of Cologne (reported by Reuter), asking for assistance in finding him a German wife. 'This is dashed embarrassing,' exclaimed the corporal when told that his letter had been published. . .

It was during the latter part of the 1930s that Hilary and Ralph decided they should employ a Chauffeur/Mechanic, and word of the vacancy was passed around the appropriate quarters of Mayfair. At that time, Henry Frederick Payne and his wife were anxious to move out of London and into the clean air of the countryside, their son being unwell. The offer from Mr. and Mrs. Bankes of employment in Dorset, with accommodation (in the Blandford Lodge), could not have come at a better time for them.

Obviously Mr. and Mrs. Payne would not have had the wherewithal to travel down from London to Dorset to inspect the lodge, but they were able to call upon some relatives who lived in Bournemouth to view, from the outside, the property. Unfortunately they viewed the Wimborne Lodge, and reported favourably that, although the house stood alone by the Gates to the Park, there were other houses within sight.

When the furniture van with Mr. and Mrs. Payne on board arrived at the Blandford Lodge they realized that there had been a misunderstanding. Apart from one house a couple of hundred yards away, the Lodge was totally isolated, with no electricity, and the toilet facilities were outside. It was a far cry from the comparatively elegant living they had become used to in London, but their little son was able to breathe clean fresh air, so they stayed.

By 1939 war was, to all but the politically blind, inevitable and Hilary, having attended a British Red Cross course in 'Anti Gas Training', organized lectures for the estate staff and tenants.

Mrs. Hilary Bankes, 'Daughter of the Regiment' was preparing herself and the estate for whatever the future held in store.

17

The War Years

SATURDAY SEPTEMBER 2nd 1939, and Ralph received a telegram from the Admiralty informing him that his beloved new 45-foot motor yacht, 'Ace' was being requisitioned for war service and instructing him to deliver it to Portsmouth Harbour forthwith.

War was declared between Great Britain and Germany on the 3rd September and Lt. Bankes RNVR was called up. The next day, Monday, Ralph, accompanied by 'Harry' Payne, the Bankes' Chauffer/Mechanic, delivered 'Ace' to the Dockyard. That evening a card from Hilary was delivered by hand to Mrs. Payne in the Blandford Lodge:

Dear Mrs. Payne

Mr. Bankes was able to phone to me tonight at 6.30 to say they had arrived safely at Portsmouth this morning. Payne has been made Chief Engineer and they have been given a crew of four others. Now they are safely in the Solent I shan't worry about them. I am very glad that they are together, and not far away. [*At this point the letter could have ended, but it continued*] If there is anything I can do for you at any time you must not hesitate to let me know. Yours Truly, H. Bankes

As part of the evacuation of British troops from Dunkirk during June 1940, both Harry Payne and *'Ace'* were involved in the lesser known 'Operation Cycle', which bought troops home from St. Valery and Le Havre. Having anchored off Le Havre until nightfall on June 10th *'Ace'* then sailed for St. Valery before heading back to Portsmouth.

Lt. Bankes RNVR was posted to the Portsmouth area, not the quietest place to be, but comparatively close to home. Their second child, a daughter Mary, was born during the early part of the war and by 1942 Hilary and their two children had joined Ralph together living in Lothian House, Fareham which they were renting.

Rationing was not for the Bankes family. Every Thursday a large hamper of food from the estate was dispatched by train to them. These hampers included a selection of vegetables and rabbits. Mr. F. O. Rhodes, the agent, was in constant communication by telephone and letter with Ralph and Hilary on subjects ranging from Hilary's application for petrol for her car to copies of Vols. 1 & 2, *Wayside and Woodland Blossoms* which Hilary had requested be sent to her. On another occasion Mr. Rhodes writes:

> I have been to Kingston Lacy this morning with Habashon and told him of your wishes regarding the changes of the furniture and the carpets from the large Dining Room, the Spanish Room and room 19 to be taken up and spring cleaned.
>
> I am sending you herewith some spinach seed which I hope will be sufficient for your summer use. Dukes will soon have 30 tomato plants ready for you. . .

Lt. Bankes RNVR (left) and Fred. Payne (right)
(Photograph supplied by Julian Payne)

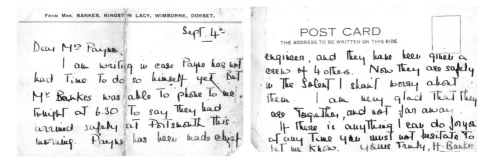

Postcard (front and back) from Hilary to Mrs Payne
(supplied by Julian Payne)

May 1942 and Mr. Rhodes in a letter to Hilary requests:

Could you kindly let me know in which week you would like the pig at
Home Farm to be slaughtered? I am asking because it is necessary to

give a fortnight's notice of the intended slaughter and no doubt you would wish your cook to deal with the usual extras from the pig.

Hilary and Ralph with the children would occasionally visit Kingston Lacy for a weekend, and Mr. Rhodes was forewarned to enable him to make the necessary arrangements to ensure the staff was well prepared and sufficient food was available.

During August 1942 Mr. Rhodes was asked, '. . . if there is any fruit we should like that sent (Not plums or apples). Also rabbits sent. I should also like 50 cabbage plants sent. . . . any further news of the Army of occupation?'

Refering to the last phrase, Mr. Rhodes replied:

As I had no further news of the 'Army of Occupation' I telephoned Major Stanford this morning and was told that it had been decided to make other arrangements. Evidently after my last interview with Stanford he was persuaded that the only probable accommodation available at Kingston Lacy was inadequate. The House would not now be required.

It was a foggy day on 24th January 1943 when a Halifax Bomber of 58 Squadron, RAF Coastal Command took off from Holmsley Airfield in the New Forest. A few minutes later it 'fell out of the sky' and crashed close to Kingston Lacy House, and all eight crew members lost their lives.

In a moving ceremony in 2000 on the anniversary of the crash attended by members of the families of the crew, together with representatives of the Canadian and New Zealand High Commissions an oak tree and a plaque mounted on Purbeck stone listing the names of the crew was unveiled close to the site of the crash by Sir Roger Palin KCB OBE Air Chief Marshal, Royal Air Force (Rtd).

Hilary and the family had now moved house and were enjoying the comfort of 'Great Brook' in Warsash. Hilary commented: 'This is a lovely house – oak beams but very up to date.'

Throughout the War people at home were always striving to maintain a 'normal' routine of everyday living, particularly for the children, and plans were drawn up to plant a tree near Pamphill Church to commemorate the Pamphill School children's success in the County Schools Trees Competition.

However a 'serious' matter was occupying Mr. Rhodes' attention:

I have to report that on Friday evening last, Dukes in company with your tenant Sergt. Chissell were successful in tracking down two men and two women apparently of the gypsy tribe who were picking snowdrops in the Lady Walk. The Police are taking up the case.

The correspondence between Mr. Rhodes and Hilary and Ralph continued on a regular basis, and during early June 1943 he wrote:

. . . and from tomorrow Dixon will send you four dozen eggs weekly. Dukes [the head gardener] hopes to send you some fair size shallots and am sending half shoulder of bacon together with one of the fattest pieces.

The following month Hilary complained to Mr. Rhodes:

. . . that the rabbits must be sent in the proper baskets, as Boast, [the game keeper] has been sending them in paper parcels and they have been arriving in a horrible state due to the hot weather.

It was about this time that the Ministry of Works requisitioned Pamphill Manor for use as a hostel for Land Army Girls and after a hesitant start, work on the building of a large hospital in the park, for the American Army, was getting under way with: '. . . about 60/70 workmen getting out the foundations for the various hutments'. However, continues Mr. Rhodes:

Corfe Castle Tolls down to £68 compared with £96 corresponding period last year. Sales of produce at the Gardens increased to £300 compared with £230 in 1942 (Jan-July) . . . I went to Kingston Lacy this morning and took 12 bottles of Port from the same shelf as before. . . they have been securely packed and put on rail today at Wimborne Station for transit to Swanwick.

In a four page letter to Ralph, written during September 1943, Mr. Rhodes gives details of estate matters, including:

Pamphill Manor now occupied as a hostel for about 30 land girls. . .
Work [on the hospital] is proceeding at a great pace and hutments going
up very quickly . . . a considerable number of men employed.

During the autumn of 1943 the family moved again, this time into
'Old Cottage' in Old Bursledon, a very traditional country cottage similar
to many on the Kingston Lacy Estate. It was not long after this that
Christmas was beginning to be discussed, Mr. Rhodes informing Hilary
that:

I have sent £2 to Mrs. Percy Tory, Shapwick, towards the children's
Christmas Tree. This is the same amount subscribed by Mrs. Bankes last
Christmas. Last year you gave the following gifts at Christmas;
Council School Prize Fund, 10/-
Pamphill Slate Club, £2
Employees, 2/6 each
St. Margaret's Inmates, 5/- each
Gillingham Inmates, 2/6 each'

During December 1943 Ralph learned from Mr. Rhodes that there
had been an:

. . . increase in wages ordered by the National Agricultural Wages Board.
Wages on the Home Farm, amongst others;
Dixon, £3-18s-0d
Cheeseman, £3-11s-2d, this includes increased overtime rates less
3/- per week cottage rent.
Cherrett (boy), £2-5s-0d
Dukes, £3-12s-0d
Thick, £3-3s-0d, after deduction of 3/- per week rent
Boast, Gamekeeper who is 75 is currently getting £2-7s-6d

The Bankes' property at that time was not confined to Dorset. During
April 1944, in a letter to Ralph, Mr. Rhodes refers to:

. . . your Cumberland property. Enclosed is a letter from the Chief Agent
(Hubert J F Smith) of The National Trust.

Re. the [Kingston Lacy] Park . . . a Board is visiting the [Hospital] site on Wednesday to give the necessary Certificate of Occupation . . . grass seed has been sown between the huts. I hope it will be possible for you to use the Wimborne Lodge entrance. I have been told that if it is possible the 'concession' will be granted to you.

Had it not been but for the loyalty of Mr. F O Rhodes to the Bankes family one wonders in what condition the estate would have been at the end of the War. This loyalty is highlighted in the following letter written, also in April 1944, by Mr. Rhodes to Ralph:

. . . several items I would like to discuss with you. I find there is a train leaving Wimborne on weekdays which will get me to Bursledon at 3.20 pm and I could catch a return train at 5.50 pm. Would next Saturday afternoon be convenient for you to see me. . . if the visit is further postponed I may not be able to travel owing to probable tightening of restrictions.

Another example of the loyalty of the estate staff is shown in the following extract from a letter to Hilary from Mr. Rhodes:

I have also seen Mrs. Sansom and she is making arrangements with Mrs. Thick to make a thorough search for any moths that may be in the cupboards and drawers and will go through the clothes and blankets. Mrs. Sansom tells me it is only quite recently that she has taken the necessary precautions in your own personal wardrobes and that she found no signs of moth.

The War seemed to be going on for ever, but for people in the South of England there were signs that something dramatic was about to happen.

18

The War Years ~ The End In Sight

D-DAY, the invasion of Europe, took place in June 1944. The hospital in the grounds of Kingston Lacy was a hive of activity, with anything up to 2,000 personnel working around the clock to treat casualties from the battle fronts.

Towards the end of 1944, Lt. Ralph Bankes was posted to Scotland, and he and the family were temporarily housed in the Roxburghe Hotel, Edinburgh.

By January the following year, 1945, the family had rented a house in Westgarth Avenue, Colinton, on the outskirts of Edinburgh, from whence Hilary wrote:

> We all (including the cats) had a good and comfortable journey up here in spite of the Christmas crowds. We are just beginning to get straight and are very lucky to have a most comfortable house. Supplies from Kingston Lacy are arriving very promptly. When the game comes to an end would it be possible for us to have a duck and a chicken each week? (Or 2 chickens or 2 ducks). Anyway when supplies do allow of this we shall be glad to have them later when the game stops if and when they are available. I enclose a letter from John. Fortunately there seems no shortage of coal here which is lucky as it is bitterly cold and snowing. Yours truly H B
>
> PS I should like Boast to continue his weekly rabbit until further notice.

During the following March a rather sad incident took place when a lady, who was acting as the Shapwick Parish Church cleaner, wrote to the Estate enquiring if some flowers could be made available for the Altar on Easter Sunday as she could not afford to buy any. Disappointingly the reply came back that there were 'no flowers to spare'.

Throughout April and May there was much correspondence emanating from the Estate Office concerning missing eggs!

The War in Europe formally ended on 5th May 1945 when the German Armed Forces surrendered to Field-Marshall Montgomery, the papers having been signed the previous night.

Everyone was anxious to 'get back to normal', and in a long letter written in July to Ralph in Scotland, Mr. Rhodes commented on a number of items concerning the estate, one paragraph of which mentioned:

> Kingston Lacy Hospital. There are now no patients at this hospital and it is practically closed down – although a fresh lot of US personnel (including coloured men) have arrived to take charge of the site and look after the German Prisoners of War (about 250 in all).

Late in July, trunks were being forwarded to Scotland as, 'We hope to come back to Kingston Lacy about August 16th . . . but as Mr. Bankes will still be in the Navy this may or not be temporary, ' wrote Hilary.

Henrietta had spent most of the war years living at 61 Brook Street, London, and in a letter to Mr. Rhodes sent during August she stated that:

> I shall be glad to have one dozen eggs once a fortnight and one bird (duck) once a month. The duck sent last week only arrived this afternoon and had to be thrown away at once owing to the transport delays and the extremely hot weather. . . the yanks have taken over the whole of Mayfair and they get everything. None of us here at 61, Self, daughter and two maids have had any eggs for two weeks.

Back in Scotland the Bankes children were, according to Hilary. '. . . wildly excited about returning to Kingston Lacy. . .'

For the average person the euphoria of 'Winning the War' soon died down with shortages of fuel, continued food rationing, and the 1947 winter the worst in living memory. The temperature did not go above freezing for nearly three months and, on a number of occasions, -20C was recorded.

But for Hilary and Ralph Bankes and their children one would suspect that life was not too bad. They were altogether and at home.

19

Dark Clouds

B Y 1950 Hilary was getting involved again in the life of the community in and around Wimborne, having been appointed Commissioner for the Wimborne and District Girl Guides.

Nationally, the 'Festival of Britain' held in 1951 was another step by the nation in its struggle to build a 'Land Fit for Heroes', and the declaration by King George VI of the commencement of the event was one of his last high profile public appearances. The following year the King died in his sleep, and his daughter, Princess Elizabeth, succeeded to the Throne as Queen Elizabeth II.

Coronation year, 1953, began the New Elizabethan Era with an air of cautious optimism. However on the 24th March, Queen Mary, possibly Henrietta's and many others' rôle model, died.

At this time Daphne was very worried about her mother, Henrietta; 'she is still very weak', wrote Daphne in a letter to Mr. Rhodes, the agent.

June 6th, Coronation Day with much celebration, and rain, and with immaculate timing we learnt that Mount Everest had been conquered for the first time by Edmund Hillary and Sherpa Tensing Norgay, members of a British-led expedition.

Henrietta's health continued to deteriorate and later in the year she was admitted into St. George's Hospital in London, where on 29th November 1953, she died, just nine days after the anniversary of her husband, Walter's death. There was a short entry, four lines, in the 'Deaths' column of the *Daily Telegraph* dated 3rd December, but no obituary.

It must have been about this time that Hilary realised that there was something not quite right with her own health. Occasionally she moved in a slightly uncoordinated way and was diagnosed as having

Ralph and Hilary receiving Corfe Castle Band, 1953
(Photograph supplied by Mrs Sybil Rhodes)

multiple sclerosis, then as now incurable and with little or no relief from the symptoms available at the time. She was eventually confined to a wheelchair and after many years being cared for at home she entered a nursing home in Ferndown, from where Ralph would take her out in his car for short rides. It was on one of these trips, on 11th September 1966, that her condition suddenly deteriorated. It would seem that he drove her directly to Christchurch Hospital where, according to the death certificate she was 'Found Dead'.

There was a simple statement in the *'Echo'* announcing Hilary's death, and she was buried in Stone Lane Cemetery, Wimborne, the funeral service at St. Stephen's, Pamphill having been attended only by close members of the family.

Within twelve months, Ralph's sister, Daphne, had died and she was buried in the same cemetery, although she spent most of her later life living in Studland.

With John and Mary having left home and living their own lives, Ralph spent the next fifteen or so years leading a quiet private life, although not, as is sometimes said, as a recluse. He was by nature a shy man, not acting or even dressing in such a way as to draw attention to himself. On a number of occasions contractors employed by the estate found themselves engaged in conversation with a quietly spoken gentleman, and not realizing that they were talking to 'Squire Bankes'.

But that era was coming to an end.

20

An Era Closes

R ALPH DIED on the 19th August 1981 and was buried next to his Wife Hilary.

John their 'son and heir' died in 1996 and was buried in Studland. So ended the dynasty of the 'Bankes of Kingston Lacy and Corfe Castle'. Why their son, John, did not inherit the estate is a matter that, it is hoped, will remain a private family matter, remembering that Mary, his sister, continues to lead her own very private life.

When visiting the house and estate one is constantly reminded of Henrietta's contribution to the long history of the locality. A large number of houses, cottages and farm buildings all bear the distinctive plaque, with the letters HRB together with a date, indicating that they were built during the minority years of Henry John Ralph Bankes, under the direction of his mother, Mrs. Henrietta Bankes.

As was said in the introduction there is very little material evidence of Hilary's life spent at Kingston Lacy, Struck down with one of the cruellest of diseases, she was denied the opportunity of carrying on the rôle of guardian of the home for her children, and probably in her dreams, her grandchildren and generations beyond. However many of the older tenants on the estate, when reminiscing of those years, recall a lady who, although firm in her approach to life, was kind, considerate and caring – which is a fitting epitaph to Hilary Margaret Bankes, the last lady of Kingston Lacy.